RURAL CREDIT

Rural Credit

Lessons for Rural Bankers and Policy Makers

K. P. PADMANABHAN

INTERMEDIATE TECHNOLOGY PUBLICATIONS 1988

Published by Intermediate Technology Publications Ltd,
103/105 Southampton Row, London WC1B 4HH, UK.

© Intermediate Technology Publications Ltd, 1988

ISBN 1 85339 020 8

Typset by J&L Composition Ltd, Filey, North Yorkshire
Printed in Great Britain by A Wheaton & Co, Exeter

Contents

DEDICATION

To the thousands of rural bankers in
the Third World countries who want to
do their job much more efficiently,
creatively as also joyfully.

Foreword

What is – and what should be – the role of rural credit in developing countries? There are two main views. The 'banking school' emphasizes the importance of financial viability of lending institutions, removal of subsidies (including cross-subsidies), and mobilization of savings. The 'development school' emphasizes the need to steer rural credit into productive projects, and into the hands of the rural poor.

Mr. Padmanabhan is well equipped to steer credit officials and policymakers through this debate and towards sound practical conclusions. His village origins, and his experience in rural banking and its supervision, incline him initially towards the 'banking school'. Unsound loans, forced upon an inexperienced farmer for a dubious technology, do not commend themselves as a cure for his or her poverty. Cumulating defaults, often encouraged by pseudo-populist promises of debt forgiveness, bankrupt the lending institutions and benefit mainly big farmers, not the poor.

But Padmanabhan also sees the force of the currently less popular arguments of the 'development school'. Officials, unless themselves steered, will find it attractive to steer public (and private) loans to richer borrowers, not necessarily to more productive ones. Reforms along 'banking school' lines, in improving on the past financial weakness of rural credit institutions, should not lose sight of their economic strength: that, since the late 1950s, they have supported much successful agricultural development. World Bank evaluations and impact studies show that its rural credit projects persistently enjoy higher economic rates of return than its other rural or agricultural activities. Yet the 'banking school' is right that such achievements will prove fragile – and non-replicable – if the lending agencies are bankrupted by excessive credit subsidy, or by failure to mobilize rural savings. ('Mobilization', however, should not be confused with mere switches of savings, e.g. from informal to formal institutions.)

Padmanabhan considers these issues as a practitioner, seeking to help his colleagues from his own experiences – and with comparisons from many countries. Seekers after a neat 'academic' analysis, with clear conclusions as valid for credit in Madagascar as in Mongolia (or Mars?), will be disappointed, and deserve to be. The credit climb, towards shared development *and* viable banking, still continues; the climbers are still learning. This is not a theory of mountaineering, but something rarer and more useful: a practical report from the rock face.

Michael Lipton
Institute of Development Studies
University of Sussex
September 1987

Preface

As the title indicates, this book is primarily intended to draw some lessons for the practising rural bankers in the Third World countries. Its contents would also be useful for those concerned with rural credit issues in donor agencies, governments, central banks, nongovernmental agencies, and academic institutions.

During the course of my career as a rural banker, I have had the privilege to interact with several of them at different layers of bureaucracy: from the field level bank worker to the Minister concerned with rural credit policy. They were indeed a heterogeneous group, some very dedicated, knowledgeable, and creative, many others frustrated, indifferent, baffled, or ignorant. One common thread that seemed to run among most of them was their relatively limited exposure to experiments outside, other than those with which they were directly or immediately involved. I remember the remarks of the chairman of a bank with a substantial rural credit portfolio when I presented him with a copy of my last book, *Rural Financial Intermediation*. In all innocence he queried, 'What is this Rural Financial Intermediation all about?' Coming from the same clan, I can appreciate his predicament: when you have so much on your desk to clear every day, you have neither inclination nor time to comprehend the ever increasing, often esoteric academic literature. Somehow, you come to assume that they are meant for the committed academic, the long-haired, star-gazing tribe, with plenty of time on their hands for debate and writing which are not of much practical value. (Indeed, some academics with very limited feel of the field did nothing to dispel this notion; on the contrary, by making excessively silly and impractical suggestions they reinforced it!) In a way this book is a modest attempt to provide a bridge necessary for that link between these two groups.

Over the past several years Rural Credit has emerged as a powerful policy instrument to deal with the problems of rural development in the Third World. Formal institutions in these countries purvey approximately US $40–50 billion annually as rural credit. Not less than 5 per cent of this comes from donor agencies. If one reckons the credit extended by the informal sector, the figure would go up by several times. It is my feeling that emphasis on rural credit by both national governments and donor agencies will continue in the coming years and that in the process they may have to face new challenges and problems. This is because the majority – often an overwhelming majority – of the people in most countries of Asia, Africa, and Latain America live and seek their livelihood in the rural areas. Most of the world's poorest of the poor are among them. Over the years, not only do we not see any perceptible improvement in their living conditions, but often they have slipped back. Any lever which can trigger a process of hope for them should not be allowed to atrophy. Rural credit is one such lever, rather a potent one at that. Also there is now an increased awareness of the widening gap in the living standards between the developed and developing countries and a feeling of obligation to the other part of humanity. (Lloyd Timberlake noted, in his book *Only One Earth*, that the estimated cost of maintaining a British cat at $260 a year, is more than the average annual income of the one billion people living in the world's fifteen poorest nations.) In this environment donor agencies are likely to look for policy instruments like rural credit that can set things at least partially right with least cost. The substantial flow of aid for this sector in fact indicates the popularity of rural credit projects among donor institutions. However, it is important that they realize the essence of the Chinese proverb: 'Don't give them fish; teach them how to catch fish.'

Writing this book, however, has not been easy. Somehow I had a feeling that I had bitten off much more than I can chew. Professor John Kenneth Galbraith has noted: 'First-rate writing meant facts, however they might be arranged or misarranged for effect.' Prodded by this dictum, I searched for facts which took me to well over one hundred rural credit projects/programmes in an attempt to draw a "Winner's" profile. I discovered that rural credit programmes are so intimately intertwined with the whole development process, that studying them in isolation or as independent segments would be difficult. Often I was like the proverbial carpenter who, summoned to repair a broken door, began to think of the door's relation to the plan of the house, that of the house to the street, street to the town, town to the country, and ended up with the broken door untouched. Drawing firm boundaries was not easy and in the process I stumbled several times on the frightful 'writer's block'.

Also, it baffled me to discover that many simple and obvious things were never put into practice for some unfathomable reasons. I was reminded of a chance remark by Professor Hans Singer: 'Don't assume that because they are simple and obvious they would be necessarily done. If that were so, development would never have been such a complicated process.' How true it is. It dawned on me that politics is inseparable from economics. Major policy changes cannot happen simply by the realization of their relevance by administrators alone. In fact, when economic costs are diffused and political benefits more immediately visible, rural financial markets can become an easy target for political intrusion. For example, the first thing a newly elected State Chief Minister in India did on assuming office, was to remit all formal loans up to Rs20,000 due from landless labourers and other rural poor. It is like an indulgent parent giving candy to the ailing child as a substitute for the medicine prescribed by the doctor. Hidden trade-offs of such all-pervasive debt repudiation would never be known, and this is no solitary case. Of course, it would be unfair to single out politicians for pursuing vested short-term interests; they seem to surface at lesser or higher degrees at other layers of bureaucracy too, right up to the field level officials.

Just as a healthy mind can only be in a healthy body, healthy credit can be dispensed only by a healthy credit institution. Hence, the litmus to test rural financial policies, in my view, is their contribution towards this end. The concept of 'counselled credit' has greater appeal to me than the conventional 'supervised credit' with a 'holier-than-thou' attitude. Money is the best extension worker and if rural financial institutions can show a better way of managing rural people's financial resources, they become more deeply rooted in the rural community. I also come to appreciate better the importance of technology as a prelude to credit. Keynes (see *Economic Possibilities for our Grandchildren*, 1930) said that the world possessed even two thousand years before Christ almost everything which really mattered – language, fire, domestic animals, cereals, the plough, the wheel, the oar, the sail, leather, cloth, minerals, banking, statecraft, mathematics, astronomy, and religion. Yet it was only from the eighteenth century that the world saw progress which gathered momentum later on. Technology and accumulation of capital were the two engines of growth. The same seems true for the developing countries of today.

As a boy in a small South Indian village, I had observed with a sense of curiosity the ways in which my grandfather lent money to poor villagers around. His ingenious ways of assessing clients, structuring his loan packages, mixing hard and soft practices to recover loans, etc. have stuck in my mind. More than all that, what made a deep impression on me was his acute common sense and abundant practical wisdom. The book that I have written is indeed a far cry from those days. But at the end of the day, aren't they still the qualities which make a successful rural banker? I have no doubt.

The book is written for both those who read cover to cover and those who dip. For the latter the chapter headings will provide useful guidance. Finally, I am not pretending that I have provided final or finished answers to rural credit problems. Far from that. By synthesizing some of the experiences, I have only tried to open up a new horizon for my fellow rural bankers who are not as fortunate as me with time. The purpose of this book will be more than served, if at least some of them who read it , are able to do their job much more effectively, creatively, as also joyfully.

A major word of thanks

For every book written, the author owes much to many, many people, who made a dream reality, an abstract idea a written work. This book is in no way an exception. My only problem is to list all those who helped me in numerous direct and indirect ways during the course of the year (from September 1986) I spent at the Institute of Development Studies, University of Sussex, as a Visiting Fellow.

Of course, my major thanks go to the IDS and all its staff. I have no doubt that, but for the stimulating intellectual environment vibrating at IDS, it would not have been possible to complete this book. Many people at IDS encouraged me in different ways. Professor Michael Lipton was indeed kind to take time to go through the draft and pen a foreword: I am thankful to him for that. Professor Hans Singer was my immediate neighbour at IDS. Through our numerous conversations across the lunch table and at other meetings, he opened up a new horizon for me: I am grateful to him for all that. The others at IDS whom I want to thank are John Oxenham, Robert Chambers, Jack Gray, Mike Faber, John Toye, Martin Greeley, Simon Maxwell, Jeremy Swift, Charles Harvey, Richard Longhurst, Reg Green, Henry Lucas, Felicity Harrison, and Ann Segrave.

John Kenneth Galbraith wrote to me blessing my second venture at writing, as was the case with my first one. I thank Galbraith for that.

The others outside the IDS to whom I am indebted are Dr J.D. von Pischke (World Bank), R.C. Malhotra (IFAD), James Copestake (University of Reading), H.J. Mittendorf, Peter Hendry (FAO, Rome), and Jean Dreze (LSE).

But for the constant encouragement of my wife Raji, both from India and in England, I suspect I would have given up the project half way through. The enormous burden of keeping our children and family going fell on her which she bore rather sportingly. I owe her a lot and only hope that such demands will not be repeated.

To be away from one's own family and people for a whole year is in itself a demanding proposition. For making it tolerable at least partially, I am indebted to Mrs Audry Swartz in whose house I lived in Brighton. I thank Audry and her children Aron, Shasha, and Maurius for their numerous conversations.

Ann Watson, Nadine and Sue Saunders did the rather unpleasant job of transcription from my not very decipherable hand. I am grateful to them for doing an excellent job.

My thanks are also due to Intermediate Technology Publications who undertook the publication of the text.

Finally, as they say, I alone am responsible for all the contents of the book.

K.P. Padmanabhan,
Institute of Development Studies,
University of Sussex, UK
September 1987

CHAPTER 1
The Process of Financial Intermediation

Money is like a sixth sense, without which you
cannot make a complete use of the other five.
SOMERSET MAUGHAM

MONEY WAS invented by man because barter was a cumbersome, wasteful, and inefficient way of making exchanges. With money came claims on money in the form of financial instruments. They are indeed a marvellous invention that permit a wide variety of heterogeneous commercial transactions with minimum transaction costs. Without them, it would be impossible to pay for goods and services, to save, and to make investments. It was the increased availability of financial instruments that facilitated the emergence of trade and commerce over the centuries. Indeed, economic growth owes much to money, deposits, loans, and financial intermediation.

Financial intermediation is a relatively simple phenomenon. It is a process where an *intermediary obtains claims* on real resources from some individuals or institutions in the community and then *re-lends these claims* to some other individuals or institutions in the community. This kind of passing back and forth of contracts among individuals and institutions who want to exchange real resources is the crux of financial intermediation. An intermediary specializing in this exchange is essential, as the contracting parties themselves are uninterested in (or incapable of) taking the trouble of effecting a contract with someone unknown to them. Essentially, an intermediary provides contacts for such contracts, and in that process benefits the economy in several ways.

Individuals, institutions, and households in any community have different income flows and investment needs. Some households find that they produce more in a given period than they wish to consume. They may find other available production opportunities unattractive. To such people, the intermediary provides financial instruments to hold their surpluses, which would otherwise have been either consumed or put to low-return activity. On the other hand, there may be firms or individuals who are unable to capitalize on attractive investment opportunities for want of additional real resources: the intermediary enables them to buy the saver's claims on real resources, through a loan. By this process the financial intermediary *transfers real resources from producers who realize low marginal return to producers who have higher returns at the margin.* This results in more efficient allocation of resources in an

1

economy, provided the cost of such intermediation is not excessive when compared with the benefits.

Firms and households in rural areas are heterogeneous and they have many different investment and consumption alternatives. They may experience excess or shortage of liquidity to respond to these opportunities. An effective financial intermediary should be able to even out these fluctuating cycles as illustrated below.

Farmer A, who lives ten miles to the north of town T, is elderly and wants to save for his old age. He owns a farm and is satisfied with his current consumption, but expects a low return on further investment in his land. He has surplus funds, which he wants to keep safe and earn a decent return.

Farmer B lives ten miles east of town T. He is middle-aged and very enterprising, but because floods affected his current yields, he has no cash surplus. Otherwise he is a very profitable farmer. He wants to own a power tiller.

Farmer C, living ten miles south of town T, is young and has inherited a farm with good yield potential. He wants to use high yielding seeds and fertilizer to boost yield potential, and would also like to improve his standard of living, but he has money only for seeds.

Under these circumstances, if a financial intermediary sets up an office at town T, accepts deposits from farmer A and lends to farmers B and C, the results would be as follows:

1.   Farmer B would be able to buy a power tiller and C would be able to buy other inputs.

2.   Farmer A would find a safe place to keep his money and earn a decent income on savings during his old age.

3.   Intermediary would benefit because the difference in interest paid by B and C on loans and received by A on deposits would more than cover the costs of loaning and servicing deposits.

4.   Society will benefit from increased agricultural production by Farmer B and C.

Without a financial intermediary none of these would have happened. Distance and lack of information would have made it impossible for A, B, and C to make face-to-face contact. Even if they were to meet, A would not be willing to risk his savings on C. Transaction costs of such direct contacts would also be higher, reducing the returns to both A and C. Specialized functioning places the financial intermediary in a better position to assess the risks associated with the production by farmer C and to collect back the money from him, thus protecting the savings of farmer A. The financial intermediary is also in a better position to alter

2

lending terms corresponding to the risks associated with lending. Thus financial intermediation is an answer to the transaction costs associated with the direct contact between surplus and deficit units. 'The crucial variable which determines the terms of lending to each class of borrower relates to transaction costs – the administrative costs plus the default risk. The fragmentation of the capital market – phenomena of different markets for different "product", – arises because of the varying transaction costs with respect to different classes of borrowers. The progressive integration of these markets is brought about through financial innovations that tend to reduce these costs. These innovations reduce the costs of lending and borrowing (costs as determined by the terms of lending) and thus bring about shifts in the supply–demand schedules for credit. It is thus that potential saving and potential investment become actual through the transmission channels provided by the integration of the capital markets. The principal variable is, of course, the risk; financial innovations tend to reduce risk.'[1]

In reality, however, rural cash flows are much more complex, varied, and heterogeneous than the one presented in the illustrative example. The presence of numerous activities in the farm and non-farm sectors and in households in different stages of life, composition, and levels of income affords a very fertile environment for financial innovation, experimentation, and intermediation to suit different preferences and needs.

Inter-regional transfer of claims

Many rural dwellers may want to send money to the city to meet their obligations. A draft from a financial intermediary is very convenient for such transfer of money from one place to another. Without such a facility they would have to carry their farm produce or money to the city, which is both costly and risky, and entrusting funds to other persons may involve loss of secrecy. The relative anonymity, convenient instruments, and safety of intermediaries can be of much help under these circumstances.

Risk management

Agricultural production is often a gamble in rains. Vagaries of weather, product price fluctuations, droughts and other natural calamities contribute to the uncertainties of agriculture. This apart, the nature of the production cycle demands an uneven pattern of expenses; for example, production expenses may be heavy during the planting season while incomes are concentrated after harvest. These variations and fluctuations in sources and uses of liquidity make it difficult for rural enterprises to manage their cash effectively. Loans and the deposit services of the financial intermediary can be of great help in managing these risks least expensively.

Term transformation

The intermediary can pool a large number of small-sum, short-term deposits and provide a few needy with lump-sum and long-term loans. The scale of operations of the intermediary allows this transformation of the term of these claims. The saver gets a return without sacrificing much on liquidity. A steady flow of short-term deposits helps the intermediary to provide long-term loans which help farmers to acquire major assets, consumer durables, etc. without having to wait for accumulation of their own savings.

Intergenerational transfer of claims

Similar non-synchronization is also present between an individual's needs and means over his productive life. A young man would like to own assets and consumer durables which can not be met by his current income. In traditional societies this problem was handled by extended families where young people could borrow from the most productive elders. Today financial intermediaries have taken over this function by financing young people's education, consumption, etc. Similarly, in the past old people who ceased to be productive depended on the young. Today, instead, they can save in financial forms and reap the benefits during their retirement period. Without financial intermediation, such synchronization of cash flows for people at different points of their life cycle would not have been possible.

The rural financial market in a country is constituted by all those who take part in this process of rural financial intermediation. It includes formal institutions like commercial banks, development banks, co-operatives, etc., agencies in the informal sector like money lenders, and all rural households who supply surplus cash to lend, or demand it as borrowers. The concept of a rural financial market embraces all the sets of relationships between buyers and sellers of financial assets who are active in rural economies. As mentioned earlier, such relationships arise from borrowing, lending, and transfer of ownership of financial assets like debt claims and ownership claims. Debt claims represent promises to pay, while ownership claims give the holder rights of control. All formal or informal evidence of indebtedness represents debt claims. Deposits are debt claims of depositors on financial institutions. These claims denote retrievability by one from the other: deposits can be retrieved *by the depositor from the bank* while loans can be retrieved *by the bank from the borrower*. Financial intermediation allows pooling, transfer, and disaggregation of these claims through time, space, and people. It facilitates a shifting of funds from areas with underutilized resources to areas with under-exploited opportunities.[2] Its usefulness increases rapidly as rural households begin to specialize in production, diversify consumption, and make large investments. In other words, as the economy progresses demand for financial intermediation increases.

In summary, it may be stated that economic development both depends on and contributes to the growth and diversification of financial intermediation. Financial services integrate markets, encourage savers to hold a larger proportion of their wealth in the form of financial assets than as unproductive inflation hedges, and allocate investible resources more efficiently. Financial deepening is achieved by reducing risks and minimizing transaction costs through exploitation of economies of scale and scope, professional portfolio management and diversification, systematic collection of information, and fostering a better lender–borrower relationship.

CHAPTER 2
The Role of Credit in Rural Development

Neither a borrower, nor a lender be;
For loan oft loses both itself and friend,
And borrowing dulls the edge of husbandry.

SHAKESPEARE

THERE IS a common misconception that if only sufficient agricultural credit were made available to farmers, the lagging agricultural sector could be regenerated. This belief stems from the basic misunderstanding of the concepts of 'credit' and 'capital'. Many reckon the two as identical concepts and assume that through additional supply of 'credit' additional 'capital' necessary for development can be created. David H. Penny has noted: 'Governments see credit programmes as an easy way to increase the flow of capital to the rural sector, but they forget that credit does not necessarily represent capital. Capital is not created merely by increasing the supply of money, nor can capital be used developmentally if farmers are permitted to use their borrowings for consumption.'[1]

'Capital' means a stock of wealth which can be used in further production, as distinguished from goods which are used for current consumption.[2] In agriculture, 'capital' represents a host of items like machinery, livestock, irrigation systems, farm buildings, well developed land, etc. In fact, the more developed the agriculture, the more would be the capital used and created by the farmers. By judiciously combining his labour with more 'capital', his productivity both per unit of labour and per unit of land increases. This increased productivity is reflected in the generation of more produce and more income.

If agricultural development is our aim we have to find answers to the following questions. How can we increase the stock of capital? And how can this be combined efficiently with the available labour and land so as to increase the productivity of participating farmers?

The fact is that 'capital' can be increased only through saving part of what is produced. If a society uses up all it produces for current consumption, there will be nothing left for making 'capital' to increase further production. So someone, somewhere, has to defer consumption. Although saving takes place in the form of money, its effect is reflected in the addition to the stock of goods. The second problem is much more intricate and complex. Over time, farmers in traditional settings have acquired amounts of 'capital' that are consistent with their technology, land, buildings, and labour capacity. In this 'equilibrium' they cannot use any additional 'capital'. The view propounded by T. W. Schultz that

6

in traditional agriculture 'capital' is not a significant constraint on the output of small farmers is now widely accepted. This low-level equilibrium can be broken only when there are profitable investment opportunities. Such opportunities arise under the following conditions.

1.   An improved technology which is clearly superior to traditional methods has been developed.

2.   Farmers understand it and are confident of using it in their field conditions.

3.   The associated support services and infrastructure facilities are present.

It is at this time that 'credit' can play its role by providing the needed liquidity to farmers who do not have sufficient investible funds to exploit the opportunity. Credit is defined as 'a condition which enables a person to extend his control as distinct from his ownership of resources.'[3] In fact 'credit' itself represents the savings mobilized by intermediaries or government from the community. Through such 'credit operations' financial savings are transformed into capital. But if 'credit' is extended without a clear opportunity it will end up as additional consumption instead of 'capital'. As Professor John Kenneth Galbraith has noted: 'At a certain stage in agricultural development, agricultural credit clearly does become a strong force for further improvement – when a man with energy and initiative who lacks only the resources for more and more efficient production is enabled by the use of credit to eliminate the one block on his path to improvement.'[4]

The foregoing presents a simplistic relationship between 'credit' and 'capital', which must be qualified in many ways.

1.   Some new technologies require no additional credit when their cost of operations is relatively small. Similarly, some rearranging of existing production patterns may need no additional credit and yet it may increase yield.

2.   In certain cases, farmers adopt new technology even without credit. These are mainly better-off farmers who are in a position to self-finance and assume the risks associated with the change. This happened in India during the early stage of the Green Revolution in the 1960s.

3.   If the cost of technology is too high, when compared with the benefits and risks associated with it, farmers may not adopt it even with the availability of credit. What worries an individual farmer is the realistic economic potential rather than the claimed technical potential.

In sum, it may be stated that 'credit' is neither essential nor sufficient to promote rural development. But financial systems can act as a strong secondary force under certain conditions. According to Hugh T. Patrick 'The financial system can influence the capital stock for growth purpose in three major ways. First, financial institutions can encourage efficient allocation of the stock of tangible wealth by bringing about changes in its ownership and composition through intermediation among various types of asset holders. Second, financial institutions can encourage efficient allocation of new investment by intermediation between savers and entrepreneurial investors. Third, they can activate an increase in the rate of accumulation of capital by providing increased incentives to save, invest, and work.'[5]

Against this perspective, it may be worth while to discuss some of the basis characteristics of rural credit.

Command over resources

Although farmers report a 'need' for credit, it is clearly not a need in the same sense as physical inputs like fertilizer, seeds, pumpsets, etc. Credit is not an input into the production process as these ingredients are. Money obtained through credit provides a command over resources and thus removes the financial constraint, if it was present prior to receipt of it.

Credit is not income

Just as money is not wealth, credit is not income, although credit could lead to income. What is important is the borrower's 'debt capacity', i.e. his ability to pay back a given sum borrowed, after putting it into productive use (see Chapter 8). When lenders and borrowers do not see credit in this light, it leads to problems for both.

Credit is fungible

Fungibility[6] implies that different units of a commodity are perfectly interchangeable. Since credit is received in the form of money it has the same properties as money. Standardization enables money to serve as a 'numeraire' and medium of exchange and makes monetized transactions more efficient than barter. Fungibility renders it difficult to evaluate the impact of credit programmes.

Credit gravitates to borrower-preferred activities

Resources obtained through credit tend to flow towards activities where the borrower has maximum preference. Priorities as visualized by the borrower are given precedence over the stipulations of the lending agency, irrespective of the type of control the latter exercises over its borrowers. This makes direct intervention by governments in credit markets through administrative fiats often ineffective. For the same reason financial institutions which meet only the partial credit needs of farmers fail to make an impact.

Need for mutual confidence

Confidence is fundamental to finance. Absence of mutual confidence between borrowers and lenders increases transaction costs. More effective interaction between borrowers and lenders would increase confidence, and consequently reduce defaults and transaction costs. When both borrowers and lenders see and reap the benefits of participating in the intermediation it reinforces confidence.

Reduced price pushes up demand

The price of credit is the interest payable. The issue of fixing the appropriate price for capital is very complex and is widely debated (see Chapter 5). As in the case of any other commodity, when the price falls demand for credit increases and vice versa, but more than other commodities, money is fungible and can be put to a number of uses. Consequently the pricing of credit has a much wider impact across the economy.

CHAPTER 3
The Evolution of Rural Credit Policies

*Economists consist of two groups: those who
don't know, and those who don't know that they
don't know.*

ANONYMOUS

THE AGRICULTURAL credit policies of many developing countries were
initially conceived as part of colonial economic policy. The promotion of
commercial production to supply the colonial power was its main goal,
so credit for tropical plantations and other such ventures was provided
by metropolitan financial markets while farm production for local
markets received hardly any institutional credit. These principles
of state intervention established in the colonial era influenced post-
independence rural credit policies.

Beginning in the 1950s, development strategies in these countries
emphasized increase in agricultural production, helping the poor, and
meeting the basic needs of rural people as their principal aims. A
number of operational programmes were tried to achieve these objectives. It is in this context that rural credit programmes came to be
implemented in these countries. Lack of economic growth was seen as a
consequence of shortage of physical capital. A vicious circle of low
capital, low productivity, low incomes, low savings, and consequent low
capital seemed to be operating in rural areas. Rural credit was perceived
as an instrument which could break this circle. The traditional urban
financial institutions like commercial banks, insurance companies,
etc. were not found suitable to provide credit in rural areas. Their
objectives, organizational structure, branch networks, and lending procedures severely restricted their ability to serve the rural sector. Consequently much of the formal credit supported by donor agencies in the
early fifties and even later found its way to more commercially oriented
producers. Except in Taiwan and South Korea, small farmers were
excluded from rural credit programmes.

Before the end of the fifties there was a marked shift in the strategy of
national governments and donors in favour of the small farmer producer.
Rural credit was viewed as the major limiting factor for small farmers in
achieving higher production and productivity. It was thought that credit
provided by informal lenders was exploitative and expensive for the
small farmers, and it was argued that this hold of informal lenders
should be counteracted by extending low-interest institutional credit.
The prevailing view was summarized by J. L. Walinsky.

Farmers in the developing countries are generally hampered by high interest costs for short-term crop loans usually from small-scale private money lenders, and by the almost complete lack of sources from which they can borrow the longer-term loans they would need to purchase draft animals and equipment, upgrade their stock, reclaim acreage, execute soil conservation measures, build barns, and finance similar capital needs. High cost loans constitute a major charge against their current income from money lenders and depress their living standard. The unavailability of longer-term credit prevents them from improving and expanding their output. Both limitations can be overcome by a well-designed agricultural credit program, at the core of which would be an agricultural bank.[1]

Against this background, in a typical small farmer credit programme an external aid agency or national government funded the estimated investment and production cost through the central bank of the country, to commercial banks/development banks, for on-lending to small rural producers. These financial institutions extended to farmers production as well as investment loans. The expectation was that with the additional physical resources obtained through loan funds, combined with the surplus labour, these borrowers would be able to increase their outputs and incomes, and repay their loans and pay interest out of the additional income. The interest charged by the financing institution was expected to cover its loan transaction costs, defaults, and capital erosions on account of inflation. Loan capital originally provided was to become a permanent revolving fund to re-start the credit cycle again. This was the model which was tried during the 1960s.

By the late 1960s, however, many evaluations of rural credit programmes threw up some disturbing conclusions. They had found a major portion of the additional credit had not reached the small rural producers, at whom all these endeavours were directed. It also became clear that many financing institutions were not able to meet their operating costs from the interest income. Many others failed to recover large amounts of outstanding loans. Overall, the assumptions of the traditional model proved to be oversimplified and they did not stand the test of time. By the mid-seventies outstanding rural credit in developing countries was around US$90 billion as shown at top of next page.[2]

Much of the credit was still provided by informal systems, particularly to small farmers. Except in Taiwan, Korea, and Colombia formal credit had reached less than thirty per cent of farm families (see Table 1).

These developments somewhat disturbed the donors and they started seeking remedies to some of these problems which had become by then all-pervasive. This led to a comprehensive review of rural credit systems in the developing world by USAID. Beginning in March 1972, more

11

	US$ billion
Funds provided by aid agencies (World Bank, Inter-American Development Bank, and USAID)	5
Funds provided by national governments	10
Funds from informal lenders	75
	—
	90
	=

than sixty project evaluation reports from thirty-seven countries were developed, from which twenty-one 'Analytical Papers' on specific themes were prepared. (The whole collection came to be known as United States Agency for International Development, *Spring Review of Small Farmer Credit,* vols 1–20, and it remains the largest collection of field studies ever assembled on rural credit.) During 1974 and 1975 small farmer credit reviews and seminars were organized by the World Bank,[3] Food and Agriculture Organization,[4] and Rockefeller Foundation.[5]

These reviews[6] and discussions brought out essentially the following issues:

1.   Design and implementation of rural credit programmes are much more complex than was hitherto thought. The traditional simplistic model can no longer be valid.

2.   Rural credit, although important, is but one of the many development services necessary for rural regeneration. If credit is to be effective, it should be supported by improved technology, infrastructure, inputs, extension, and markets. In other words, it is not the type of credit organization that alone is important, but the economic opportunities associated with rural credit.

3.   The viability of financial institutions serving small farmers could be eroded by low interest rates, high administrative costs associated with administering small loans, and cumbersome banking practices inappropriate to the needs of small farmers.

4.   Most, if not all the economic, social, and political difficulties that have retarded overall agricultural development also hinder the development of credit institutions which serve small farmers.[7]

The Spring Review commented on AID small farmer credit programmes:

Table 1: Credit from institutional sources

Country	Percentage*
Africa	
Ethiopia	1
Ghana	1
Kenya	12
Morocco	10
Nigeria (western)	1
Sudan	1
Tunisia	5
Uganda	3
Asia	
Bangladesh	15
China (Republic of Taiwan)	95
India	20
Jordan	8
Korea, Republic of	40
Malaysia	2
Pakistan	5
Philippines	28
Sri Lanka	14
Thailand	7
Turkey	23
Vietnam, Republic of	21
Latin America	
Bolivia	5
Brazil	15
Chile	15
Colombia	30
Ecuador	18
Guatemala	2
Honduras	10
Mexico	15
Nicaragua	20
Panama	4
Paraguay	6
Peru	17

* Families receiving rural credit to total farm families
Source: World Bank, Agricultural Credit Sector Policy Paper; May 1975, p. 71.

The US technicians have tried with perhaps too much enthusiasm to apply two US institutional models – supervised credit and co-operative credit. But the 'transplant' problem is probably less significant than some critics claim. A more serious problem was the absence of and re-examination of the fundamental assumptions underlying the small farmer programs – that government-supported institutional credit channelled through conventional mechanisms was necessary and sufficient to small farmer progress – in spite of rapidly accumulating evidence that many of the programs were not working ... The most significant conclusion of the report is that there has been and continues to be too little professional attention given to credit issues (beyond organizational and methods matters) to match the relatively high rate at which AID resources are pushed into credit programmes.[8]

Some other important conclusions of these reviews were as follows:

1.   No particular type of institutional system, be it co-operative, commercial banks, specialized development banks, or project authorities, could be termed as the preferred model for rural credit delivery. Successful institutions were those which could reach the maximum number of clients with minimum cost. This was possible through (a) decentralization of operations; (b) grouping of farmers; (c) using those intermediaries that already possess a rural network; (d) tapping local savings; (e) providing access to private institutional money markets. Group activities with an element of compulsory participation had a greater degree of success.

2.   Private co-operatives have an important role in any credit programmes for small farmers. Local participation, group sanctions against delinquency, and better use of scarce technical training could be achieved through them. The major problems in organizing these co-operatives were shortage of local leadership and the fear of certain governments of promoting local bodies.

3.   Private money lenders could be utilized as agencies by the formal lenders, to reach large numbers of clients with minimum cost.

4.   All the rural credit agencies in a country should work collectively as a mutually supporting system, retaining their particular attributes, rather than as isolated alternatives. Such a financial system should be co-ordinated with other institutions dealing with marketing, extension, and input supply to ensure the success of credit projects.

5.   It is important that financial institutions should remain viable and survive as financial intermediaries. Experience indicated that newly created credit programmes were often handicapped by incompatible

14

programme goals thrust on them. It took a long time for many institutions to develop and mature.

6. An almost universal problem observed was the insufficient number of trained professionals. A tendency to hire urban-based technicians lacking experience or empathy with the rural poor was also seen. Hiring of rural-based, project-trained para-professionals was suggested as a remedy.

7. The need for a self-evaluating mechanism to monitor progress and assess achievement of goals was stressed. Such a system could provide signals of straying and other problems as and when they cropped up.

In sum, the process of providing credit and related services to rural people was recognized as a much more complex process than hitherto thought. Devising appropriate institutional mechanisms and systems for loan administration, management information, evaluation, personnel management, supporting services, co-ordination, etc. was indeed a challenging task. The World Bank's Sector Policy Paper on rural credit summarized the problem. 'There is a need to learn much more about the most appropriate channels for providing credit at low cost to enable large numbers of small farmers to become productive. It is clear that any system intended to reach large numbers of low-income producers will have to be based on principles different from those designed to reach a relatively few large producers. In the case of grouping or co-operative institutions, their needs and their importance in the community should be properly identified and their specific nature, to be most effective, should vary according to the different societies and cultures among which they have to function.'[9]

CHAPTER 4
Why Credit for the Rural Disadvantaged?

*Credit supports the farmer as the hangman's
rope supports the hanged.*

FRENCH PROVERB

IN MOST developing countries two factors have contributed to increasing
rural poverty and destitution: high population growth and neglect of the
rural sector. In the Asian continent the population doubled during
1950–80. Between 1975 and 1987 agricultural population per unit of
crop area increased by 50 per cent in Bangladesh, 30 per cent in
India, 18 per cent in Indonesia, and 34 per cent in Pakistan. (In the
Republic of Korea and Japan, on the other hand, there was a reduction
of agricultural population per unit of crop area during this period by 19
and 55 per cent respectively.) This heavy pressure of population on
land, and lack of employment opportunities elsewhere, have already
resulted in a substantial increase of small farmers, marginal farmers,
and landless in these countries. They somehow try to seek income-
earning opportunities in farm or non-farm activities. In Bangladesh, for
example, half the rural population is landless. The bulk of the agricultural
labour in that country comes from these landless, yet this work absorbs
only about one-fifth of their total time. Eighty per cent of their labour
time is spent either in non-farm activities or in idleness. Although
Bangladesh is an extreme case, the same trend is visible in many other
countries.

The main business in the rural sector is agriculture, which supports a
large workforce. For example in India 69 per cent of the labour force
depends on agriculture. This percentage has remained unchanged for
the past three decades. Agriculture also contributes substantially to
national income, to exports, to domestic food and raw materials supply,
and to the purchasing power of a national market for industry. Whatever way one looks at growth, whether in terms of popular welfare
or industrial growth, the role of agriculture and rural development is
significant. No real development is possible in these countries without
developing the small farms which predominate in their agriculture. As
early as 1957, P. T. Bauer noted: 'The main reason for the low average
incomes in the so-called over-populated areas is the abundance of un-
skilled or semi-skilled labour relative to the available land and capital,
and often especially to land improved by the embodiment of capital.
Improvement for the majority depends ultimately on increasing the

volume of capital and skill, thus changing the ratio between the various classes of resources. The measures of reform now being examined merely alter the institutional framework without influencing the availability of resources and therefore do not get to the root of the problem.'[1]

Increased emphasis on smaller rural producers was in particular due to the following factors.

1. *Failure of past growth-oriented strategies.* The anticipated 'trickles' from development strategies involving massive capital investment were too insignificant. There was a marked polarization in the rural sector, where a small number of large producers had received most of the benefits. The consequent increase in poverty and inequality forced many governments to reorient their development strategies in favour of the rural disadvantaged.

2. *Need for productive employment.* A new strategy was needed to generate productive employment for the growing labour force in the countryside. Capital-intensive industry models developed in the Western countries were clearly unsuitable. It became evident that additional urban employment can never keep pace with the need, and that the large proportion of people will have to remain in rural areas seeking productive opportunities in farm and non-farm activities.

3. *Availability of technology.* Experience in Japan and Taiwan demonstrated that with 'Green Revolution technologies' even a small producer of irrigated rice or wheat could obtain higher yields per hectare. This increased yield and income, and consequent higher purchasing power in the hands of rural people, was expected to trigger demand for other goods and services in the rural sector. This could generate demand for non-farm activities where the rural poor could find employment.

4. *Higher productivity of small farmers.* Evidence has shown that small farmers produce more per hectare than large farms.[2] While large farms can produce more per man-year, smaller farms tend to produce more per hectare. When land is becoming scarce and labour plentiful, the strategy which encourages small farmers seems more rational. According to S. Wortman, 'All of this [new technology] is aimed at generating the main ingredient for rural development: increased income for large numbers of farm families. Until their purchasing power is increased through on-farm or off-farm employment, there can be no solution to the world food problem. Extending science-based, market oriented production systems to the rural masses can enable the developing countries to substantially expand their domestic markets for urban industry. As farm families obtain larger disposable incomes through increased agricultural profits they can become buyers of goods and services, providing more jobs and higher incomes not only on farms but also in rural

17

trading centres and in the cities. What I am suggesting, in other words, is that the improvement of agricultural productivity is the best route to economic advancement for the agrarian developing countries.'[3]

Emphasis on credit for the rural disadvantaged

Under what conditions and environments does the ability of the rural disadvantaged to participate in productive activities increase? It was clear that a host of facilitating factors were needed. A small rural producer typically used a traditional method of cultivation, he was often slow to adopt new and more productive technologies, his risk aversion tendency was found to be high, and rural services did not reach him easily. However, within these limitations he was found not averse to real economic opportunities when they were presented. It was also found that once new planting varieties and production techniques were developed, credit had greater potentialities to remove many of the associated constraints faced by the rural poor. This was found to be true for both farm and non-farm activities. This approach to supporting small farmers was advocated in 1973 by Robert McNamara: 'The miracle of the Green Revolution may have arrived, but for the most part, the poor farmer has not been able to participate in it. He simply cannot afford to pay for the irrigation, the pesticide, the fertilizer ... For the smallholder operating with virtually no capital, access to credit is crucial. No matter how knowledgeable or well motivated he may be, without such credit he cannot buy improved seed, apply the necessary fertilizer and pesticide, rent equipment, or develop his water resources. Small farmers generally spend less than 20 per cent of what is required on such inputs because they simply do not have the resources.'[4]

Dr Schultz had argued that the low productivity of farm labour was due more to the absence of credit to finance specific factor inputs. Supply of new agricultural inputs to them through credit was seen by him as the most practical way to achieve increased agricultural productivity. Financial credit is the most flexible form of transferring economic resources to the poor: one can buy anything that is for sale with cash obtained through credit. When goods and services are transferred to the rural poor through administrative allocation, the freedom of choice and efficiency available with credit is lost. Of course, the social efficiency of credit would depend on the borrower's ability to judge his needs and on whether his needs coincide with what is prioritized socially. Experience shows that provision of credit to small producers satisfies these prerequisites of efficient resource allocation.

Who are the small farmers and rural disadvantaged?

Smallness is necessarily a relative concept. In a country where all farms are small, a small farmer would be one whose land is smaller than the average size. As farm sizes are found on a continuum, any attempt to draw a firm line between large, medium, and small has to be necessarily arbitrary. The problem of identifying a small farmer becomes more complex when we reckon the yield variations of land due to differences in soils, climates, farm practices, ownership patterns, density of settlement, etc. A farmer owning a large holding in a mountainous arid region may indeed be a poor one as compared with a farmer owning a smaller holding with access to irrigation in a valley. The *Spring Review* grouped small farms into four categories.[5]

1.   Those already operating as reasonably profitable commercial enterprises with access to commercial credit.

2.   Those which have the potential to become profitable enterprises if access to technology, inputs, and markets at real prices were possible.

3.   Those which have the potential to become profitable enterprises but will need special incentives – subsidized prices – during an unspecified period of time.

4.   Those with such poor resources that improved access or even new technology would not provide a viable farm enterprise capable of supporting the farming unit.

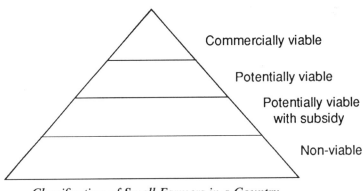

Commercially viable

Potentially viable

Potentially viable with subsidy

Non-viable

Classification of Small Farmers in a Country

The concept of viability was the principal criterion for this classification. However, viability itself could be interpreted in different ways and no uniform yardstick to measure viability was developed during the *Spring Review*. The issue was clarified by Gordon Donald: 'For the present we may conclude by noting that a small farmer can be defined as one whose resources are too small to qualify for existing bank credit. He may or may not have the appropriate growth potential as a farmer; but if he does, a way of reaching him should be found.'[6]

The International Fund for Agricultural Development uses four criteria to identify the rural disadvantaged, i.e. *regional criteria,* assuming that all households residing in that region are poor; *asset criteria,* by prescribing a cut-off level of assets and income depending on the incidence of poverty in the country; *activity criteria,* by selecting activities attractive only to rural disadvantaged; and a *combination* of any of the three above.[7] In India four different criteria have tried to identify the rural disadvantaged and these criteria varied, depending on the institution implementing the programme and the purpose of the programme. For determining subsidy eligibility under the Government of India's general programmes, farmers holding below 2.5 acres were classified as marginal farmers and those holding between 2.5 and 5 acres as small farmers. However, under its Integrated Rural Development Programme, an income of Rs62 per capita per month at 1975–6 price levels (about Rs3500 per annum for a family of five) was reckoned as the cut-off level to identify poor families. Financial institutions also followed this criterion to identify the rural poor under this programme. For other programmes they chose criteria such as the size of loan, i.e. those who demanded loans below a cut-off point were treated as small farmers. A combination of the pre-project income and land holding criteria was developed by the National Bank for Agriculture and Rural Development in India. It classified farmers into three groups: small farmers up to an income of Rs4300; medium farmers from Rs4301 to Rs7500; and big farmers above Rs7500. (This definition originated with World Bank funding in the early seventies. A small farmer was one whose net pre-development income was less than Rs2000 at 1972 prices.) Based on the consumer price index for agricultural labourers for the State concerned, this income norm was to be converted into current prices. These income levels were translated into acreage norms through field surveys. In a fertile region a farmer with a smaller holding was categorized as 'big' while in a poorer region even a much larger holding qualified him to be a small farmer.

All these methods encountered one problem or another. Choosing an entire region as backward was found operationally convenient for bank field workers and others concerned with a programme. Under this criterion even the not-so-poor residing in the area received the concessions of the programme. There were also political pressures to declare regions as backward to pre-empt programme concessions. When a cut-off point was fixed regarding size of landholding, it failed to take into account inter-regional differences in the productivity of land, and consequently many poor farmers in the arid regions were excluded. In some countries, particularly in Latin America, it was found difficult to assess

20

the total land holding due to fragmentation and uncertain claims of ownership. In many cases estimating family income was found difficult, particularly when the households had non-farm incomes. The size-of-loan criterion was easy to operate for financing institutions, but there was no guarantee that big farmers would not seek small loans and that small farmers might not genuinely need large loans. Conversion of pre-project incomes into regional acreages was also not without defects. A 15-acre large farmer in a poorer region may be worse off than a 3-acre small farmer in a fertile region at a given time, but it says nothing of the potential. Through resources obtained through loans, the former could become a very large and profitable farmer.

In summary, we could say that there is no single way of defining and identifying small farmers and the rural disadvantaged. The criteria to be chosen would depend upon the country, the characteristics of the region, and the nature of the financing agency. The criteria chosen should be unambiguous, operational, and comprehensive, so that they are easily understood by bank agents who can implement them in the field without much difficulty.

Some illustrative examples of criteria chosen under IFAD Projects to identify rural disadvantaged are given below.

Country	Ceiling Criteria
1. Bangladesh (Small farmer credit)	
Hand tubewell	2 acres
Deep tubewell	3 acres
Fish tank	2 acres
(Grameen bank)	4/10 acres
2. Dominica	10 ha (4 ha cultivated) US $2000 (for family of 6)
3. Lesotho	Not well-defined – average farm size in project area is 5 ha and per capita income less than US $160 (60% of national level)
4. Morocco	Fiscal income DH 3000
5. Nepal	1 ha in hill area 2.67 ha in Terai area Rs 950 per capita income
6. Nicaragua	2 ha (small) 2–10 ha (medium)
7. Pakistan	25 acres

Country	Ceiling Criteria
8. Peru	5 ha (farmers)
	Income equivalent to 5 ha farm
	(small livestock producers)
9. Paraguay	3.5 ha
10. Tunisia	5 ha (small)
	5–50 ha (medium)

Why is credit not reaching the small rural producers?

In whichever way one defines the small rural producer, the available evidence shows that they have very limited access to formal rural credit. In most countries, formal credit has not reached more than 20 per cent of all farmers. Roughly 5 per cent of all farmers in Africa, 25 per cent in Asia, and 15 per cent in Latin America have access to formal credit. In many countries 5 per cent of the borrowers have received 80 per cent of institutional loans. In a typical developing country the pattern has been as shown below.[8]

Farmers	Share of Formal Credit (Percentages)
1	80
15	20
84	Nil
100	100

Those excluded are mainly small farmers. For example, after reviewing the credit situation in India in 1976 the National Commission on Agriculture noted: 'An important feature of the co-operative credit had been its tendency to flow mainly to larger cultivators . . . Similarly, an analysis of the agricultural financing by the public sector banks has also revealed that farmers having holding above 2.02 ha get about 74% of the total credit advanced by banks.'[9]

Three sets of factors have contributed to this phenomenon: the preference of formal institutions to lend to big producers; the reluctance of small producers to approach formal agencies; and pre-empting of credit by big producers.

Preference of formal institutions

Formal institutions prefer lending to big producers for the following reasons.

1. Proportionate loan administration costs are considerably less for big loans as compared with smaller loans.

2. Big producers can comply with the lender's collateral stipulations.

3. Lenders view collated credit as much more secured than non-collated credit. Thus there is a greater sense of safety in the case of big loans.

4. Attaining the national objective of increased food production is more easily possible through big producers.

5. Lenders can win political patronage by obliging big producers.

6. Completing predetermined loan targets is much easier through lending to big producers.

7. The poor are often seen as unreliable clients due to their unstable and small incomes, and their irregular savings and borrowings.

Reluctance of small producers

Small rural producers are reluctant to approach formal institutions for the following reasons.

1. There is a perceptible cultural gap between the formal lenders, mostly originating in the urban environment, and the rural borrowers who are accustomed to a different way of borrowing money.

2. Information relating to various credit schemes, formalities, obligations, etc. do not reach small producers, particularly when they are illiterate.

3. Small producers located in remote rural areas find the formal institutions with restricted banking hours and days not easily accessible to make their financial transactions.

4. Various terms and procedures of institutionalized lending are inappropriate to the needs and cash flows of small producers.

5. They also find it difficult to comply with several loan formalities like filling of loan applications, obtaining guarantors, etc. insisted on by formal lenders.

6. The flexibilities needed by a small producer for repaying the loan are not built into formal loans. This makes him fearful of the consequence of non-repayment to a formal lender.

7. Credit from formal lenders is tied to pre-identified production activities, whereas for a small producer his immediate consumption needs are more pressing than productive investments. Formal lenders, however, view consumption credit as unproductive.

8. For a small producer, credit from a money lender, although at a high interest rate, is often readily available round the corner, in a system to which he has been accustomed for generations.

Pre-empting by big producers

Institutional loans are pre-empted by big producers for the following reasons.

1. The big producer has a range of profitable opportunities in both rural and urban areas to deploy funds. Funds from formal institutions are attractive for him, especially when they are offered at relatively low rates. He could obtain loans for the purposes stipulated by the lenders and divert his own funds to other avenues.

2. Big producers have better access to information on various credit and subsidy schemes due to their nearness to banks and other contacts.

3. Conforming to collateral and other requirements of lenders is much easier for a big producer.

4. He can also afford the delays and incidental charges associated with formal loans, unlike a small producer.

5. Big producers also find it lucrative to obtain formal loans and then relend to needy small producers who are reluctant to approach formal lenders directly.

In summary, it may be stated that formal loans reach few small producers in the developing world. Yet it is on them that governments depend for food and raw materials production. Ways have to be found to improve their outputs and living standards. The questions we have to ask are: Are these distortions inevitable in a rural financial market? Can we create vibrant rural financial institutions without these distortions? What are the associated problems and possible solutions? What are the success or failure stories of some of the rural credit experiments around the developing world? What lessons can we draw from them for changing policies and procedures? The rest of this book is addressed to these questions.

CHAPTER 5
The Current Debate on Rural Financial Markets

There is no truth; there are only ways of seeing.
GUSTAVE FLAUBERT

THE THEORETICAL basis for a 'pump-priming approach' in rural credit came from Hugh T. Patrick.[1] The establishment of financial institutions and provision of loanable funds in advance of established demand were seen as effective levers to promote rural development. The funding of a large number of rural credit projects and the building of many new rural financial institutions, particularly in countries like Brazil, India, Jamaica, Mexico, Thailand, and the Philippines, were the result of this approach.

Assumptions under traditional policies

Traditional rural finance policies were based on the following assumptions.

1. Credit was the major constraint which prevented rural people from pursuing their chosen activities and on the adoption of new technology.

2. Rural people were required to pay higher interest rates than willing to meet this credit shortage, particularly to the informal lenders.

3. This led to exploitation by the monopolistic money lender, further impoverishing the rural poor.

4. The concessionary institutional loan was seen as a helping hand to counteract these vicious forces.

5. Interest rates were a critical factor in borrowing decisions as they contributed the bulk of borrowing costs. Consequently, demand for credit by rural people was assumed to be interest-rate elastic.

6. Poor rural households have limited savings capacities.

7. Formal financial institutions could effectively ration and direct funds to target groups and activities, by enforcing strict loan supervision, by granting loans in kind and through other controls.

8. Since credit for consumption was likely to be misused, formal lenders were not to provide such unproductive loans.

9. Adverse effects of pricing and exchange rate policies could be offset through subsidizing interest rates.

25

Effects of these assumptions

Rural credit programmes which operated on these assumptions met with the following problems.

1. Many agricultural banks and development institutions, created exclusively to lend to the rural disadvantaged, floundered around the developing world. Their agricultural portfolios were eroded by high inflation and fixed interest rates.

2. Many of these institutions could not reach the rural disadvantaged for whom they were meant.

3. Loan delinquencies and defaults emerged as a serious problem.

4. Many institutions started resenting any involvement in the rural sector except with big clients. When they were mandated to lend to small producers they either tried to circumvent the regulations or concentrated on the better-off of the small producers.

5. Serious management and organizational problems emerged in many banks. There was a shortage of competent and trained personnel.

6. A tendency to concentrate on short-term production loans as against long-term investment loans was visible.

7. Most of the banks did not mobilize voluntary rural savings. The few who mobilized these savings, siphoned them to urban areas.

8. Rural financial institutions depended heavily on central banks or donors for resources. This paved the way for political intrusion in them.

9. The single major factor which contributed to the erosion of their profits was the high lender transaction costs of small loans which could not be covered through interest income. Hence, in their struggle to keep afloat, these institutions found ingenious ways to transfer part of the transaction costs to their actual or potential borrowers.

10. This further weaned small people from institutional loans. The benefits of formal loans, such as income transfer due to negative real interest rates, non-repayment of loans, etc., were in effect reaped by big borrowers who could participate in financial intermediation.

11. Overall these distortions led to the emergence of badly fragmented rural financial markets.

The new approach: retrospect and prospect

Without fully realizing these implications, policy makers and rural bankers created new state supported agencies, or reorganized the existing ones which had failed to lend to the rural poor. Some of the private institutions were nationalized. They were asked to lend a fixed portion of their total portfolio to specified activities, target groups, and/or areas. Several other restrictions on size of loan, clientele, etc. were also imposed. Loan guarantees and insurance cover were provided to reduce the risks of lenders and borrowers. Institutions which complied with these regulations were made eligible for more concessionary refinance and capital subsidies.

Criticisms of the validity of this approach came from David Penny[2] (on the basis of his experience of small farmer credit programmes in Indonesia) and Dale Adams[3] (on the basis of his experience of credit programmes in Latin America). They found that some of the basic assumptions relating to finance on which these measures were based were questionable. There was evidence to show that adoption of new technology did not necessarily depend on the availability of credit. In their view the 'villain of the piece' was low interest rates, to which many governments in developing countries were committed. Low-priced credit generated excess demand, necessitating rationing. This led to corruption and political intervention to get 'sweet money' which was pre-empted by big borrowers. While a few people got more credit than they needed, many genuinely needy were starved. Low interest rates on lending forced these institutions to offer lower rates on savings and with this source not tapped, they had to depend on external agencies for funds. Much manpower had to be spent in meeting the donor requirements of reporting. Low interest rates gave banks low margins and consequently they could not offer a variety of services needed by rural clientele. On the demand side, they found that as credit provided additional liquidity, it had an impact on all activities of the borrower and not only on the one financed by the bank. This rendered assessment of the impact of credit difficult.

Based on this evidence, the new approach outlined the following strategies:[4,5]

1. Evidence suggests that there is far more liquidity in rural areas than is generally assumed. This is partly due to seasonality in agricultural production. Moreover, rural people are responsive to interest rate changes and appropriate financial services. Hence, mobilization of voluntary financial savings in rural areas should be the first priority of financial institutions.

2. Mobilization of savings would enlarge the resource base of lending agencies and correspondingly reduce their external dependence. It would also reduce loan defaults as borrowers would be more careful with neighbours' savings than with government funds.

3. Offering higher interest rates on savings deposits would be possible only if the rate of interest on loans is raised. Such charging of positive

real interest rates reflecting the general scarcity of capital would revive the repressed market forces and allow the allocative and regulatory function of interest rates to operate freely.

4. Increase in lending rates would also give financing banks higher operating margins to meet the transaction costs of lending to small farmers. When such lendings become commercially attractive, credit will flow automatically to the rural poor without any external compulsions and mandates. Higher lending rates would also make it unattractive for big farmers to pre-empt institutional loans. Thus small farmers have better prospects for getting formal credit when interest rates are high.

5. Interest forms only a small part of the total cost of borrowing by the small farmer. Even now, the so-called cheap institutional loans are not that cheap, if the borrower transaction costs of getting official credit is included. Hence, from the point of view of small farmers, credit from the informal sector, which has much lower borrower transaction costs, would often work out cheaper than formal credit. In these circumstances, they would be willing to pay a higher interest rate to formal lenders if the borrower transaction cost were reduced. In their relative effects on farmer behaviour, product prices rank first, yields second, input prices third, and credit availability and interest rates constitute a distant fourth.

6. Higher interest rates would enable the banks to offer a range of financial services needed by the rural community. Through such services and deposits far more people could participate in financial intermediation. Consequently, these institutions will become better integrated with the rural community.

7. When market forces are revived, targeting of loans and supervision of compliance therewith, will no longer be necessary. Anyway, due to the fungibility of money, additionality, substitution, and diversion that occur because of a loan are hard to assess. Reduced emphasis on loan supervision will cut down the lending costs. Borrowers will be more prudent while using resources when costs are high. Thus increased reliance on farmer rationality would work in the interests of both the borrower and the lender.

8. The village money lender will continue to remain a valued source of credit in rural areas for a long time because of his easy approachability, informality, and flexibility. It would be better if formal institutions learned from the money lender rather than treating him as despicable. A workable arrangement for co-existence between formal and informal lenders would be in the interests of the rural poor.

Overall, the new approach assigns a major role to interest rates in stimulating rural financial markets.[6] Finance is to be viewed as a process of intermediation rather than as an input for production. The critical issue relates to improving this process through reducing the cost of intermediation, increasing the dependability of the lender, and providing appropriate services, not to finding solutions to individual lender problems. Allowing the revival of market forces instead of direct controls can be more effective in achieving these objectives. This is because market forces exert a powerful impact on the allocation of claims on resources, regardless of policy-makers' philosophical orientation. Dale Adams summed up the new strategy.

Despite the confusion that surrounds rural financial markets, the treatments for its problems are relatively simple. First and foremost much more emphasis must be placed on encouraging rural financial markets to mobilize savings ... It will also be necessary to revise interest rate policy ... High rates on loans would reduce the demand among those who use large amounts of cheap credit, allow more lenders to cover their costs and encourage lenders to reduce the costs of transacting loans for both borrowers and themselves ... Policy makers should not try to accomplish too much with credit projects. Product prices, crop yields and the costs of production are much more powerful determinants of farmers' decisions than are credit availability or interest rates.[7]

However, there are several problems in putting this new approach into practice in the rural financial markets of developing countries. Recommendations relating to wholesale changes in the interest rate policy are never implemented *in toto*. This is because interest rate and foreign exchange rate are the two most important prices in any economy. Any changes in them have repercussions across the economy and would affect several other sectors and programmes, including borrowings by government. Also, it would not be feasible to have a separate interest rate structure for rural financial markets: if attempted, it could lead to uneconomic diversion of resources as well as leakages between sectors.

The precise role of interest rates in the economic development process is a subject which has been debated considerably over the past four decades since Keynes. Differing viewpoints have emerged as to the way in which this instrument has to be deployed. The debate on interest rates among policy makers, aid agencies, and academics has become so complex that separating the different strands of thought has been like untying the Gordian knot. The term 'interest rate' means different things to different people – savings deposit rate, lending rate, price of capital, cost of funds, rate of return, etc. The search for a 'pure', 'real', 'optimum', or 'equilibrium' interest rate is, according to Professor Boulding, meaningless, like looking for a non-existent black cat in a dark room. Some argue that economic transformation can occur only when agriculture is capitalized and excess farm labour is shifted to the industrial sector. They view low interest rates as a way of encouraging such capital intensification. On the other hand, a recent study in Sri Lanka concluded that interest rate policy alone cannot bring about any change in either savings, investment, or inflation.[8]

Financial markets are often depressed due to distortions in other segments of the economy, which in turn may have been due to political considerations. Under these circumstances, rural financial market reforms would not be possible without corresponding economic and political adjustments for which many countries may not yet be ready. Moreover, for better or worse, farmers have been used to low-interest formal loans for a long time. Ironically, even those few small farmers who receive formal credit would severely protest against any increase in interest rates, let alone the big farmers.

Further, although an upward revision of interest rate is recommended, it is often unclear as to what would constitute an optimum level of interest under different conditions. In the process of removal of repression it would be unwise to swing the pendulum to the other extreme. Allowing a free play of market forces would not necessarily meet the equity objectives in an economy with marked inequalities in income, wealth, and skills. As Michael Lipton has pointed out: 'The mainstream institutional approach to rural credit has in most cases achieved little, at high cost. Appropriately sweetened, the tough market medicine advised in the new consensus might in theory help, since inappropriate incentives (such as tolerated default and subsidized interest) benefit mainly the richer and less efficient users and suppliers of credit. But in practice it is for that very reason, in most cases, that these powerful men seek and successfully maintain such incentives. Therefore an attack on their power – through radical structural reform, whether distributive or collective – is probably in most cases a necessary condition for improved incentives and markets in rural credit as elsewhere.'[9]

Central banks would continue to support and regulate rural financial institutions. When they provide funds for on-lending, they are likely to stipulate that a specified portion should be lent to the rural disadvantaged. It may also not be wise to rely completely on farmer rationality for loan utilization. Some sort of counselling or contact by the lending institution with the borrower as to how he deploys the borrowed funds seems essential, in the interests of both borrowers and lenders. In other words, although one cannot work against the market forces, these very market forces could be influenced in favour of the poor through appropriate incentives and interventions. Any proposal to reform rural financial markets will have to reckon these realities and opt for only a gradual change, making the most of the existing constraints. Some of these issues are dealt with in Chapter 13.

30

CHAPTER 6
The Structure of Financial Institutions

If you want to understand the causes that existed in the past, look at the results as they are manifested in the present. And if you want to understand what results will be manifested in the future, look at the causes that exist in the present.

SHINJIKAN BUDDHIST SUTRA

SEVERAL types of credit institutions – some nation-wide and others regional-based – have been tried in the formal sector to supply credit for rural activities. They include national development banks, specialized agricultural credit institutions, commercial banks, rural banks, co-operatives, government supported project authorities, etc. Their appropriateness and effectiveness have depended upon several factors. A single institutional model suitable to all countries does not exist – no one structure could be said to be clearly preferable to others. What is important is that these institutions should be able to adapt to local conditions and financial flows. Generally, credit institutions have an apex financial agency under which several layers of bureaucracy operate. At the bottom is the widely dispersed organization which delivers credit. These agencies at the bottom are responsible for the day-to-day operations of granting, supervising, and collecting loans. The four major types of organizations are commercial banks, agricultural development banks, co-operatives, and project authorities.

Commercial banks

Commercial banks were the earliest formal agricultural credit agencies in most developing countries. They were financing particularly large farmers, as well as various agricultural supply and marketing agents. Later on some commercial banks started extending more credit to small farmers, partly on account of government compulsion and mandate. For example, in India until their nationalization in 1969 commercial banks had only lent Rs2580 million to agriculture, which was just 7.1 per cent of their total credit. By September 1985, their lending to agriculture had increased to Rs81,740 million, constituting 18.1 per cent of their total credit. The branch networks some of these commercial banks had built over the years in these countries were useful in expanding their rural credit operations, and with their professonal expertise in financial management and huge resource base, they could extend a range of services to clients. However, most of them did not take to rural lending wholeheartedly. Their penetration to rural areas and financing of farmers,

31

particularly small farmers, received only a left-handed treatment. This was because of their concern to increase profits and to reduce risks, both of which were found difficult in rural lending. Born in urban environments, they also found it difficult to adapt to local cultures and ethos. Donor agencies have used commercial banks as conduits for their funds. Central banks have provided concessional funds to commercial banks for lending to agriculture. For example, in Mexico, the Bank of Mexico (Central Bank) provides rediscount facilities to commercial banks and to a government development bank for medium and long-term agricultural loans. By providing guarantees, concessional refinance, and technical assistance for training, the Bank of Mexico encourages commercial banks to lend to small farmers. In India, the Reserve Bank of India (Central Bank) extends concessional loans to the National Bank for Agriculture and Rural Development for on-lending to small farmers through commercial and co-operative banks. Such concessional refinance support to rural credit is being extended by other central banks, particularly in Asian and Latin American countries.

Agricultural Development Banks

Most of these banks were established in the past 20–25 years for dealing exclusively with farmers and other rural communities. One notable exception is the Agricultural Bank of Turkey which was established more than 100 years back. Some of these development banks, for example the National Bank for Agriculture and Rural Development (NABARD) in India, act as an apex refinancing institution for co-operatives and other credit agencies in the country. Some of these institutions lend directly to the farmers and extend their area of operations to the whole country. The National Agricultural Credit Bank (CNCA) in Morocco has a system of regional banks lending directly to medium and large farmers along with a large number of local banks lending to small farmers (see Chapter 8). The Agricultural Development Bank of Pakistan, the Bangladesh Krishi Bank, the Bank Rakyat Indonesia and the Agricultural Development Bank of Nepal are some examples of development banks operating nation-wide and lending directly to farmers. Many of these development banks are either fully owned by the State or have substantial State participation. Some of them originated due to availability of counterpart food aid funds, an example being the Agricultural Refinance Corporation (which later on became NABARD) in India, set up in 1963 with PL–480 funds. The major drawback of some of these banks has been their excessive centralization, often making them ill-suited to lend to highly dispersed small farmers. Excessive centralization in some of them has resulted in increased administrative costs, and inability to adapt to local conditions. Many of these development banks depended heavily on government funds and consequently political intervention in them had become a rule rather than an exception. J. D. von Pischke commented on their performance. 'Unable to act as a rural institution intermediating between rural savers and borrowers, it serves merely as a one-way link between the government and rural sectors. Rural people are not regarded as a market to be developed, but are seen as poor, exploited, or economically incompetent people requiring assistance. Rural people, in turn, do not view specialized farm credit institutions as something of their own, but as a benevolent intrusion to be exploited. In these circumstances a specialized farm credit institution is not well positioned to learn about rural financial flows, behaviour, and local priorities – knowledge available only to those who enjoy sufficient rural confidence.'[1] Unfortunately many development banks have fitted this description.

Co-operatives

Unlike commercial banks and development banks, co-operatives sprang up in rural areas. In many areas, they were the most accessible formal system for farmers, in particular small farmers. Co-operatives had the feel of the local area, reflecting the rural ethos and culture. Farmers felt at ease with the loan agents of co-operatives, unlike in the case of commercial banks. In addition to credit, co-operatives were built around several other functions such as supply of inputs, marketing of output, managing of storage or processing facilities, etc. Many co-operatives had their own apex bank, and local co-operatives were linked to the apex bank through a district/regional association. In some countries co-operatives were linked to a national agricultural development bank or the central bank. Despite the potential advantages of the system, building effective co-operatives for credit delivery has been found difficult in many countries. The main problems faced by them were paucity of trained personnel and informed leadership. In many cases, e.g. village credit facilities in India, they could not attain a level of business which could make them viable. Political interference and pre-emption of benefits by big farmers were often found in co-operatives. The major problems of co-operatives in Africa were (a) absence of experienced management (Zambia, Tanzania, Ethiopia and Zimbabwe), (b) uneconomic base level units (Tanzania, Zambia), (c) lack of supporting infrastructure like extension, training, etc. (Zambia, Zimbabwe), (d) poor member participation due to hasty launching of co-operatives, (e) insufficient supervision and auditing of co-operatives (Zimbabwe, Zambia, Tanzania), and (f) too much political disturbance (Zambia, Tanzania and Ethiopia). When co-operatives undertook a variety of activities, the management was not found competent to carry them out. When one of the components failed, it affected the entire co-operative. For example, in cases where marketing and credit were combined, failure in marketing led to failure in credit delivery, due to an increase in loan defaults. In the case of co-operatives in Cameroon, although they were partly successful in credit operations, they were failures in marketing, inputs supply, and extension. Because of this, concentration on a single activity by co-operatives is often recommended. Bruce L. Robert Jr. summed up the position relating to credit co-operatives in India: 'Ostensibly begun to establish small scale credit institutions for the poor, they had within a quarter century evolved into a large bureaucratic structure. This growth was the result not of its economic merits, but of its political influence. The inequities of the rural socio-economic structure worked to exclude the poor and place the rural rich in a dominant position in the movement which became a useful "patronage bank" of considerable utility to politicians.'[2,3]

Project authorities

A system which is rather less frequently used for credit delivery is a project authority. Such authorities have been established to execute projects such as those relating to land settlement, crop development, irrigation, and credit is added as an additional function. Often they are government departments, public boards, statutory corporations, funds set up by special acts, etc. This has been tried mostly in countries/ regions which did not have a well-developed rural banking system. They have worked as a satisfactory channel for reaching relatively large numbers of smallholders in Africa. Some of them could provide a guaranteed market for the crops of small farmers and thus link credit with marketing. They could undertake delivery in kind to borrowers. Some of them could offer supporting services. However, they are found to have high operating costs as compared with other banks. Their experience in loan collection has been mixed.

Thus different credit delivery institutions have been tried in different regions. Co-operatives, private or state-owned rural banks, and commercial banks are more prevalent in Asia. In Latin America the preference has been for government-owned development banks and rural co-operative societies. In Africa, although government-owned agricultural credit institutions have been given priority, their effective spread has been rather limited due to the wider geographical dispersion of farmers and a shortage of middle level bank personnel. Revolving funds as part of rural development projects have been tried in Africa to provide short-term production credit. In the Near East region, governments have promoted agricultural credit through co-operatives and specialized banks.

Overall, it can be seen that the depth of formal financial intermediation is determined by the level of development of a country. The least developed countries have a relatively small rural financial system. As their economies expand, their financial systems respond by playing an increasingly important role in the efficient allocation of resources. Thus we observe three levels of financial institutions: relatively backward, as in the case of some African countries; middle level, as in the case of some Asian countries; and an advanced level, as in the case of the Republic of Korea.

Institutional development is a long and difficult process. Hence it is preferable to develop or reorganize or strengthen an existing financing institution instead of creating new institutions. However, wholesale changes in the institutional structure, and abrupt mid-course corrections could be counter-productive, because it takes considerable time to understand the full implications of any institutional restructuring.

Moreover, in most of these countries, past state interventions during the colonial era have set a pattern for their institutional structure and any changes have to be necessarily gradual. Trying to achieve too much in too short a time may be counter-productive, as noted by an Indian rural credit study. 'Too many and too abrupt changes in policies relating to agricultural credit should be avoided, particularly as such credit is dispensed on a decentralized and diversified basis in "Lakhs" of villages. It is, moreover, appropriate to allow sufficient time for the policies now under implementation and experiments now in progress to work themselves out for some time and throw up lessons for the future.'[4] Whatever may be the structure of the lending institutions, their success would depend on the following factors:

1. A clearly specified and consistent institutional objective and a system which assesses the achievement or otherwise of those objectives.

2. A decentralized system of operations with a high level of efficiency in mobilizing resources, loan administration, and recovery of loans.

3. An ability to create a sense of confidence in the rural clientele, and to adapt to existing rural culture, institutions, and leadership.

To achieve this, it may be necessary to try different types of credit institutions in different parts of a country. Looking for a perfect model applicable to all areas may be futile. It may not also be possible for a single institution to offer all the services needed by the rural clientele. Even in countries like the Republic of Korea and Taiwan, where one officially sponsored institutional structure has succeeded well in meeting the credit needs of a wide variety of rural activities, other agencies, particularly informal finance, have fulfilled certain other felt needs. Thus co-existence of different kinds of financial institutions catering to different financial needs may be necessary depending on an individual country's circumstances. It is, however, good to remember that what is more important is the overall performance of the rural financial market in a co-ordinated and efficient way than individual excellence by certain institutions and in certain areas. As R. L. Meyer writes: 'It is unlikely that a single type of rural financial institution will be optimal for all LICs. Each country must develop a mix of institutions consistent with its particular needs with emphasis on two criteria for institutional development. First, multi-functional institutions that link savings and credit activities should be expanded. This involves strengthening the lending activities of specialized savings institutions and the saving mobilization activities of specialized lenders. Second, a range of institutional forms must be provided to meet the needs of a specific rural market'.[5]

Some of these issues relating to institution building are discussed in Chapter 13.

CHAPTER 7
Mobilization of Resources

*The principle which prompts to save is the desire
of bettering our conditions, a desire which though
generally calm and dispassionate, comes with us
from the womb, and never leaves us till we go to
the grave.*

ADAM SMITH

FUNDS FOR investing in agriculture in the developing countries come
from three major sources: public investment, private investment, and
foreign aid. The share of public investment would be roughly 70 per cent
in a typical developing country, private investment at around 10–15 per
cent, and the balance of 10–15 per cent from foreign aid. To meet these
investment commitments, governments mobilize resources partly through
land revenue, agricultural income tax, betterment levies, and import/
export duties. Household savings are the major source of private investment. The shortfall in the mobilization of domestic savings, both public
and private, is met by foreign aid and investment.

A minor chunk of this large pool of resources is channeled through
financial institutions for investment in agriculture and rural development. For example, when a government undertakes to construct an
irrigation dam, it constitutes a direct public investment. But when it
contributes to the share capital of a financial institution which lends to
farmers for undertaking irrigation investments, it becomes an indirect
public investment. When farmers self-finance farm investments it constitutes direct private investment. On the other hand, when they choose to
save and keep deposits with financial institutions who lend for farm
investments, it becomes an indirect private investment. The funds of
financial institutions come from this aggregate pool, private savings, and
foreign capital, in the following forms:

(*a*)   Equity capital contributed by government, private agencies, or
donors.

(*b*)   Accumulated reserves and retained profits.

(*c*)   Borrowings from central banks or governments or donors.

(*d*)   Other borrowings from the capital market.

(*e*)   Deposits mobilized from the public.

Although the share of these different sources varies from institution to
institution and from country to country, two general trends have been
visible in the structure of these resources, firstly a heavy reliance on
concessional funds from central banks or aid agencies, and secondly, a
relative neglect of savings mobilization from the public.

The eagerness of aid agencies to support credit programmes in developing countries has encouraged this tendency to rely on external funds. Aid agencies on their part have found rural credit projects as a convenient mechanism to channel large funds relatively quickly. Also there has been a common belief that mobilizable rural household savings were very meagre, and if they existed at all they were too costly to be institutionalized. A common impression was that poor people had no savings. Although it is common wisdom that agriculture must provide resources for other sectors during the early stages of development, mobilization of deposits is seldom given priority. It is now becoming increasingly clear that to create healthy rural credit institutions, their continued dependence on foreign savings should come down. Similarly, when governments mobilize resources for financial institutions through involuntary techniques such as taxes, inflation, price ceilings etc., the resource allocation efficiency suffers.

Mobilization of voluntary deposits is the most effective way to expand lending operations without foreign dependence. Thus of the five resources mentioned earlier, this is the one with vast untapped potential.

Scope for mobilization of rural savings

The Third United Nations International Symposium on 'Mobilization of Personal Savings in Developing Countries', held in Cameroon in 1984, concluded that domestic savings existed in most developing countries on a larger scale than was generally thought. Two studies, one by Alexander Muser and another by Sung-Hoon Kim, conducted for the symposium confirmed this.[1] The latter study, which covered eleven Asian countries, found that over the past few years there had been a steady increase of between 9 and 25 per cent in savings in money over savings in kind in every country, with a faster rate of increase in rural than in urban savings, especially in South Asia. The Grameen Bank experiment in Bangladesh (see Chapter 9) demonstrated that the poor would save as much as 50 per cent of additional income, under appropriate conditions. Likewise it was found that during 1982 in Mauritius the average size of nearly 470,000 savings accounts was $30.48 while in Peru the average size of 5 million accounts was $87.27. In fact evidence shows that rural people save proportionately more than urban people. In India, during 1961–62 rural households with an annual income range Rs4800–7200 saved 19 per cent of their income, while urban households with an income range of Rs6000–10,000 saved only 11.4 per cent.

While discussing rural savings, it is essential to distinguish between savings made by abstinence from consumption and savings in the form of financial assets, which represent one form of holding a stock of savings. A decision to hold financial assets may or may not affect aggregate savings. The potential for rural savings arises on account of the following factors:

1. Abstinence from consumption is necessary for survival even for the very poor. Consequently, poor households do save although the amounts are small and the time period for which they are retained is short.

2. There is divergence between production and consumption cycles, particularly in rural areas. This creates 'liquidity cycles' which offer scope for savings. Thus savings represent temporary liquidity not immediately spent on receipt (and not the residual funds left over from consumption during a given period).

3. Rural households are heterogeneous in source of incomes, stage of development, surplus generation, and consumption needs. This heterogeneity offers opportunities for financial institutions to even out between surplus and deficit households, through collection of savings.

4. Marked inter-regional differences in resource endowments, technology adoption, and income generation offer scope for mobilization of surpluses.

5. In some developing countries, remittances from abroad by migrants from rural areas offer scope for savings mobilization.

Institutionalization of rural savings

There are two sides to mobilization of rural savings: the *Supply Side* – the circumstances under which rural clientele are most likely to entrust their savings to financial institutions – and the *Demand Side* – the efforts and range of services of financial intermediaries to institutionalize surplus funds. The following factors influence institutionalization of rural savings.[2]

Economic environment. The extent of monetization in an economy is a crucial factor in deposit mobilization. When farmers produce for markets, their ability and willingness to interact with the market, particularly with financial institutions, increase. On the other hand, during high inflation and economic instability rural households would prefer physical assets to financial savings.

Generation of income. Savings are positively related to income, although the exact relationship between them is not clear. The experience under several credit projects proves that the marginal propensity to save by the rural poor is very high. When credit-promoted activities generate additional income, they could be tapped as savings by financial institutions. Although higher income households also save, they are more sensitive to the returns earned from financial assets. Also they have, unlike low income households, access to a wider range of investment opportunities, including physical assets like land, jewellery, etc. Low income households need the services of financial institutions, particularly when they receive 'lumpy' incomes to be consumed over a period of time. Field studies carried out for the 'Cameroon Rural Finance Sector Study, 1986', found that coffee, cocoa, and cotton farmers who receive their incomes once a year, had to keep their savings in cash all through the year due to lack of financial institutions.

Confidence in the institutions. Confidence is the basis of any financial transaction. This is more so in the case of rural people, who are cautious in letting others have their money. Safety, continuity, and secrecy are some of the factors that foster confidence. Some government intervention may help in creating a sense of safety and confidence. When deposits are covered by insurance, it increases savers' confidence.

Interest rates. Rural people are rational in their approach to financial matters and they do take advantage of attractive interest incomes on deposits, if offered. In effect, an increase in interest rates makes current consumption more expensive than future consumption, and consequently promotes deferment of consumption. It can also be argued that, with a higher interest rate, the amount of present savings necessary for a given level of future consumption would be less. However, the evidence in countries such as Taiwan and South Korea supports the earlier assumption. When deposit rates were increased in these countries, financial institutions could mobilize large rural savings. On the other hand, in countries where real deposit rates became negative due to inflation, savings mobilization was limited. Overall, it has been found that financial deposits respond more to real interest rates than national savings, due to the substitution of financial investments for other investments.[3]

Access and range of services. Accessibility to the financial institution is an important factor in the promotion of savings. When bank branches are opened near market centres and operate at convenient hours, rural people opt to institutionalize their surpluses. When they are confident as to its liquidity, they would prefer to earn something on the surplus rather than keeping it idle. Stipulating low minimum transaction and balance limits would attract smaller depositors. Provision of financial services like money transfer from one centre to another can encourage depositors. Similarly, non-financial services like payment for the purchase of crops, payment of bills, etc. can increase deposits. Payment for crops presents an opportunity for intermediation because the buyer could establish an account payable in favour of the farmer. When there is a linkage between savings and lending, rural households will be prompted to hold deposits with a view to availing a loan when needed. A study among the women emloyed by the Cameroon Development Corporation in South-Western Cameroon, found that they did not use banks for their savings for the following reasons: high initial sum ($20) necessary to open a savings account; inaccessibility of bank (reaching even the nearest bank required a long uphill walk or costly taxi ride); each deposit involved a service fee of $0.40; low interest rates on deposits.

Transaction costs. Fees, charges, and other costs for keeping the savings influence the net return obtained from interest earned on deposits. Some of the explicit costs to the depositor are the cost of photographs, pass books, and travel. In addition there are implicit costs like time spent on travelling, waiting, etc. to make the transaction. When financial institutions impose high transaction costs small depositors become discouraged. A study in Nigeria found that simple transactions at commercial banks in Lagos took 8 or 10 times longer than in the US or UK due to faulty procedures and inadequate training of bank staff. Using thumbprints or photos for illiterate customers, labelling of counters, and such other simple procedural reforms would have markedly improved customer service.

Innovative experiments.[4] Collecting weekly deposits, as in the case of the Grameen Bank in Bangladesh, is one innovative way to synchronize demand with rural cash flows. Special savings instruments like 'savings stamps' introduced in Indonesia may be useful. Some countries such as Cyprus and Mauritius have introduced savings scheme in schools, to instil the habit of saving in children's minds. The Schools Savings Scheme in Mauritius is sponsored by the co-operative movement and supported by the government. Under the Women's Savings Club in Zimbabwe each club determines the minimum to be saved by each of its members in any given week and members failing to save this amount pay a fine of one or two cents per week. Prolonged defaulters in savings for 10 weeks are expelled. Each club maintains a savings account with a bank. The management committee of the bank inspects the club's savings book after each deposit to make sure that the entire weekly collection is deposited. A member can withdraw her savings any time at a week's notice. Mobile banks or mobile rural credit agents, as in Pakistan, can tap the deposits at the doorsteps of the people. The appointment of rural agents on a commission basis may work in some places, as was tried out by the Syndicate Bank in India through what was known as the 'Pigmy deposit scheme'. In the Republic of Niger, a savings bank has considered the system of daily deposit collection on market sites. Experience shows that well motivated bank agents can tap rural savings much more effectively. The Self-employed Women's Co-operative (SEWA) in Ahmedabad, India, had employed savings mobilizers to explain to illiterate clients the procedures for depositing and withdrawing funds. In the very first year eleven mobilizers could tap as much as Rs1.1 million through 3000 savings accounts. In areas where rural people are sceptical

41

of formal institutions, group savings could be promoted. In areas where there are restrictions on dealings by women with outside men, women employees of the banks may be utilized to tap the savings of women. In countries where religious opposition exists to interest payment other methods of rewarding the savers may be explored.

Linking informal savings clubs with banking institutions. Informal savings clubs operate in many developing countries. They are called 'Ikub' in Ethiopia, 'Dyanggy' in Cameroon, 'Chilemba' in Uganda, 'Esusu' in Liberia, 'Cheetu' in Sri Lanka, and so on. Ikub is extremely popular in Ethiopia. Even in areas where banking facilities are extensive, Ikub membership is around 60 per cent of local population. During 1968–73 around Ethiopia $200–250 million (8–10% of GDP) was estimated to have been saved through Ikubs.[5] These are grassroots-level groups which operate with rules and regulations suited to local traditions and conditions. These groups also act as a forum for exchange of information on market news, improved farming techniques, etc. Mechanisms have to be found to link these informal savings groups to formal banking institutions.[6] According to Robert C. Vogel and Paul Burkett: 'The services provided to small savers by informal financial intermediaries, such as rotating savings and credit associations, indicate that projects that attempt to forge linkages between formal and informal FIs can yield significant benefits. It would be useful to try some experimental programs oriented towards exploring the costs of such linkages and other specific innovations in financial technology in the light of the specific resource bottlenecks (e.g. skilled labour) faced by most developing countries.'

Linking savings with other services. When savings are linked to other activities like marketing, supply of inputs, extension, consumer goods, and credit, mobilization could succeed better. The Savings Movement in Zimbabwe followed such an integrated approach by linking savings to distribution of inputs (seeds, insecticides), provision of technical advisory services, and marketing. The scheme was in fact initiated by a non-governmental organization in collaboration with a fertilizer company and integrated savings with marketing of inputs and extension. Savings permitted farmers to purchase fertilizer at reduced prices, so a timely supply of fertilizer was ensured. Overall, this integration helped to increase farmer incomes and savings. Similarly, regular supplies of consumer goods to rural areas could provide an indirect incentive to savings mobilization. The experience of Taiwan in the mobilization of voluntary savings is particularly interesting. 'Household savings were strongly stimulated by two sets of incentives. The first set included price policies, new technology, marketing facilities, land tenure adjustments, and public investment programs that gave strong incentives for on-farm investments. The second set of savings incentives flowed to farmers through financial markets. The physical presence of savings institutions in most rural areas (farmers' associations, postal savings, and commercial banks) gave rural people the opportunity to save and provided convenience, stability, liquidity, and security necessary to attract savings. Furthermore, Taiwanese policy makers were aggressive in using attractive interest rates on deposits to induce savings.'[7]

In sum, institutionalization of rural savings depends on:

Ability to save: availability of surplus income.

Opportunity to save: presence of secure and accessible institutions.

Incentive to save: a condition where the sacrifice involved in saving will bring a better future reward.

Advantages of promoting rural savings

Promotion of rural savings benefits both the rural people and the banks. The availability of savings opportunities discourages unproductive household consumption for the poor while savings increase their capital and resource base and consequently their bargaining power. For the financial institution, savings increase the funds available for loaning. For many this means reduced dependence for funds on central banks or foreign agencies, and consequently less intervention by politicians and other vested interests. Savings pave the way for increased local participation in financing bodies, which makes them more responsible both to borrowers and depositors. Through savings, banks can reach a much greater number of rural people than through loans and become aware of their needs, preferences, and cash flows. Unlike forced savings through taxes, inflation, etc., voluntary savings mobilized by financial institutions permit investments to be made directly by farmers to their best advantage.[8]

Salient features of some of the successful savings mobilization schemes are discussed below.

Agricultural co-operatives in the Republic of Korea (Currency Won: W)
Primary co-operatives at the township level, county co-operatives, and the National Agricultural Co-operative Federation constitute the three-tier co-operatives structure in the Republic of Korea. More than 80 per cent of farm households are members of the primary co-operatives. Heavy emphasis has been placed on mobilization of rural financial savings by these co-operatives.

Before 1965, the nominal rate of interest on deposits in co-operatives ranged between 9 and 15 per cent. In September 1965 nominal rates on deposits were hiked up to around 27 per cent, which in effect gave a positive real interest of over 10 per cent. Consequently, the share of agricultural co-operatives in the total financial and savings deposits of the country increased as shown below.

Year	1963	1964	1965	1966	1967
(a) Contractual interest on 1 year deposits (%)	15	15	18	26.8	26.8
(b) Changes in wholesale price index (%)	20.6	34.6	10.1	8.7	6.4
(c) Real interest rates (%)	−5.6	−19.6	+7.9	+18.1	+20.4

	(Thousand million W)		
	1965	1966	1967
Total financial deposits	114.4	162.1	259.3
Share of Co-operatives (%)	14	17	14
Total savings deposits	44.6	93.9	162.3
Share of Co-operatives (%)	9	16	12

One could derive the following conclusions from the Korean experience in deposit mobilization:

1. Deposit behaviour is strongly influenced by the interest rates offered.

2. Rural people have much larger savings capacities than usually assumed.

3. A well-organized and decentralized system of co-operatives can institutionalize rural savings more effectively.

4. Government policies relating to savings promotion and interest rate affect considerably the ability of rural financial institutions to mobilize savings.

Co-operative Savings Scheme in Kenya (Currency Kenyan shilling: KSh)
The Co-operative Savings Scheme (CSS) was started in Kenya in 1970 as an adjunct of the Co-operative Production Credit Scheme (CPCS). CSS supplemented CPCS as a source of funds for lending short-term and medium-term credit to coffee farmers. These co-operatives enjoyed a virtual monopoly on smallholder coffee production in Kenya. Primary produce marketing societies participating satisfactorily in CPCS were eligible to join CSS, upon having necessary supporting facilities like trained staff, security arrangements, accounting system, etc. A novel feature of this link between CSS and CPCS was that the former operated through the individual accounts maintained by the latter for paying members for their coffee crop deliveries and for recovering loans made to them by their societies. Payments due to members for their coffee

44

produce were credited to their accounts. These amounts were allowed to be withdrawn within certain restrictions. Thus no new account was opened for a depositor and this considerably reduced transaction costs on deposit collection.

In 1972, CSS commenced operations and by 1973 it had covered seven District Co-operative Unions. Balances in around 100,000 accounts exceeded KSh36 million with an average of KSh325 per deposit account. Half of these accounts had just around the minimum balance of KSh50.

The following factors contributed to the success of CSS:

1. It addressed to the felt needs of the producers. With a low minimum balance stipulation (unlike commercial banks and post office savings) it offered a safer and profitable alternative to cash hoards by reducing liquidity costs.

2. Automatic crediting of crop proceeds to CSS accounts generated savings automatically.

3. The interest rate of CSS at 4% was only one per cent above the rates offered by commercial banks and the post office, but the farmers could avail loans in small amounts from CPCS.

4. The minimum loan limit at CPCS was KSh100, whereas in commercial banks the minimum was generally KSh1000, while the post office did not extend loans at all.

The CSS experience indicated the importance of savings–credit linkage in the promotion of rural savings. It also demonstrated that even when the time-lag between realization of income and its consumption is very short, such short-term surpluses could be institutionalized if farmers had access to appropriate savings mechanisms.

The 'Cheetu' system in Sri Lanka (Currency Rupees: Rs)
The 'Cheetu' is an informal Rotating Savings and Credit Association (ROSCA) most popular in Sri Lanka. A group of participants agree to make a periodic contribution to a fund that is given to each member in turn. For example, when there are ten participants each contributing Rs10 monthly, each member by turn will get Rs100 every month. Each time the beneficiary is chosen by drawing lots. After ten months one 'Cheetu' cycle ends. A new cycle could be started with more contributors and with different contributions or intervals. 'Cheetu' is an informal financial arrangement which ingeniously combines savings with lending. A member is a saver until he receives the fund and thereafter a borrower. In fact 'Cheetu' embraces all strata of society in Sri Lanka, in both rural and urban areas. Even very poor people organize 'Cheetu' with amounts as low as one or two rupees. The success of 'Cheetu' has the following lessons:

1.   They meet the demand for financial services in a way and scale that cannot be organized by many formal agencies.

2.   Financial arrangements that are flexible, adaptable, and accessible, and which involve simple procedures, attract all types of clients, more so the rural poor.

3.   Informal financial arrangements can accommodate savers, borrowers, and lenders belonging to poor rural households by helping to balance their uneven flows of income. Hence instead of destroying such arrangements in the informal sector, formal agencies should be encouraged to take innovative approaches that build on the positive factors of these systems.

Banco Nacional para las Co-operativas (BANCOOP) in Peru
BANCOOP is not a bank under Peruvian law, but a co-operative which performs most banking functions. During late 1979, BANCOOP initiated its savings mobilization activities in the two target offices in Huancayo and Tringo Maria. By mid-1981 these offices could mobilize deposits greater than the target of US$50,000. As a matter of fact, there was initial scepticism at BANCOOP and many had favoured mobilization of resources through demand deposits and capital contributions from member co-operatives, rather than through time and savings deposits. However, BANCOOP found that capital contributions increased loan demand in excess of their loanable funds. Demand deposits could not provide a stable source for lending. Eventually time and savings deposits became their major source of funds for lending. They were costlier than capital contributions and demand deposits. Yet BANCOOP could earn substantial profits as the interest earned on the loans was much in excess of the cost of time and savings deposits.

Several factors contributed to this substantial increase in deposits, despite an adverse economic environment:

1.   Nominal interest rates in 1981 was increased from 30.5 per cent to 50.5 per cent for savings deposits and from 35.5 per cent to 54 per cent for time deposits.

2.   Appropriate incentive schemes were devised to motivate staff for better performance. This markedly improved the quality of services to depositors.

2.   Deposit schemes were widely publicized and attractive prizes were offered for depositors. Yet the total cost of the deposit campaign and employee incentives was less than 2 per cent of the deposit mobilized. BANCOOP experience shows that confidence of depositors in the institution, prompt banking services, effective deposit mobilization campaigns, and employee morale are the key factors in successful savings schemes.

46

CHAPTER 8
Issues in Loan Administration

It is one of the complexities of the subject that
debt may be as much an indicator of prosperity
as of poverty.

MALCOLM LYALL DARLING

ONCE FUNDS have been mobilized, the next important issue relates to lending them effectively to the rural clientele. A host of factors contribute to effective rural lending.

Loan appraisal

Loan appraisal is a process of determining broadly in advance the various lending parameters for given activities within a region. Resource endowments and the availability of technology would determine the scope for different activities. The willingness of rural clients to take advantage of these potentials would depend upon their level of skills as also on the availability of supporting infrastructure, inputs, and markets for outputs. Appraisal is an assessment as to whether these conditions are present and whether these opportunities remain unexploited for want of credit. Appraisal also reveals the major constraints operating and the support needed to remove them.

The four purposes [1] for which credit is needed are:

(*a*) short-term production inputs like seeds, fertilizer, pesticides, feed, raw materials, etc.;
(*b*) long-term investments like farm machinery, livestock, irrigation, wells, land improvement, etc.;
(*c*) consumption credit to support the farm household during the intervening period of production as also contingencies like illness;
(*d*) repayment of past debt obligations.

Farm families are simultaneously units of production and consumption, and all these four components affect one another closely. Formal institutions normally try to restrict credit to the first two purposes, but money obtained through credit will flow to the most pressing of these needs. Hence the best way for a formal lending agency is to explicitly recognize all these needs and budget for them – in fact granting consumer loans seems to improve repayment of both consumer and production loans.[2] In Mexico, farmers who received credit for consumption had 10–20 per cent better repayment rates on their production loans

47

than farmers who had received only production loans. The Wolamo Agricultural Development unit in Ethiopia could also increase repayment rates by granting consumption credit during the crucial pre-harvest period.

The quantum of loan will depend upon the prevailing cost of assets in the nearby markets. Instead of absolute amounts, only a range of admissible amounts needs to be fixed at the time of appraisal, leaving discretion to borrowers to procure assets/inputs they want. The overall loan limit for each borrower will have to be based on his debt capacity.[3] Determination of a client's debt capacity requires good judgement and experience on the part of the lender. First he should quantify the normal year's uncommitted cash flow, i.e. produce prices less cost of purchased inputs. From this, essential consumption expenditure has to be deducted. Thereafter adjustments for adversity have to be made to arrive at the minimum level of repayment capacity of the borrower.

Duration of the loan and phasing of disbursement could be determined by the purpose of the loans. Loans for inputs should be short term, the exact period depending on the duration of production cycle of the crop. When loans are extended for purchasing an asset, the duration of the loan should not extend beyond the life of the asset financed. When an asset is built up gradually, e.g. for land clearing and planting of an orchard, disbursement of loan should be synchronized with the graduation.

Fixing of loan repayment schedules is an important aspect of financing. From the farmers' point of view it is more advantageous to get a longer-term loan than a low-interest loan. The repayment pattern should synchronize with the generation of cash flow under the project. Under the Grameen Bank Project in Bangladesh, for activities generating daily or weekly incomes, fixing of weekly repayments has been found very effective. When there is an initial gestation period for income realization, a repayment holiday for that period may be appropriate. In the case of poorer farmers, a larger share of income from the project should be allowed to be retained for home consumption, with a corresponding extension of the loan period. If, during the currency of the loan, the borrower experiences a crisis in the enterprise (for example loss of production due to pests) or at home (for example unforeseen medical expenses) the repayment schedule should be restructured depending on the incidence of crisis. In short the key words when determining loan amount, duration, and repayment pattern are 'flexibility', 'adaptability', and 'synchronization'.

Loan approval procedures

Within the broad norms of lending determined at the time of appraisal, loaning to individual borrowers takes place through numerous banking outlets. Loan application forms, supporting documents, collateral required, internal processing system, mode of disbursement of loan, etc. form part of the loan approval procedures.[4]

Rural borrowers view the loan application form as an irritant, especially when they are illiterate and do not fully know what it contains. An Oxfam study in Maharashtra (India) found that bank loan applications had to be supported by eight or more documents each requiring costly official stamping. Farmers had to travel 2 to 55 km to reach bank offices and an average loan involved 10 to 12 visits over a period ranging between 6 and 16 months. In addition to loss of wages during this time, farmers had to incur many other expenses like fees, bribery, cost of refreshment to middlemen, etc. This is one of the reasons why money lenders are preferred to institutional lenders. For the latter, however, lending without a formal application would not be possible. First of all they do not have sufficient information on individual farmers and even if they do, a loan officer would try to put things on record as much as possible to safeguard his interest, in case of a subsequent default. These conflicting positions can be resolved to some extent by the senior management of the bank through the following ways:

(*a*)   Stipulating a simple format for loan applications. If necessary, separate formats may be devised for different types of clients.

(*b*)   Using the local language for the application forms or providing a translation.

(*c*)   Omitting the type of information which would not be eventually used to make loan decisions.

(*d*)   Keeping the supporting documents as minimal as possible.

Insistence on tangible collateral has been the legacy of traditional commercial banking. Loans backed by personal assets like land gave a feeling of safety to the lender. Such a stipulation, however, made formal institutions inaccessible to marginal farmers and the landless. Paradoxically, in practice, banks have found it difficult to realize bad loans through sale of mortgaged land: bidders do not readily come to purchase a neighbour's land and legal procedures were found to be cumbersome. On the other hand, such insistence on collateral often contributed to avoidable distrust between lenders and borrowers. Some of the alternatives that can be tried without jeopardizing the lender's interests are:

(*a*)   Obtaining the personal guarantee of the borrower and that of a co-signee acceptable to the lender.

(*b*)   Creating a charge on the assets purchased out of borrowed funds, in favour of the lender.

(*c*)   Asking the groups to indemnify individual loans, where groups are operating.

(*d*) Simplifying the legal procedures. In Pakistan under the Loans for Agricultural Purposes Act, 1973, a pass book (in duplicate) is issued from the post office in which the Revenue Department fills in the particulars of land owned by the farmer. Lending institutions use these pass books as evidence of farmers' title to the land indicated therein.

Evidence indicates that prompt repayment depends on several factors and collateral is the least of them. On the other hand, collateral credit restricts the business of lenders by weaning away many otherwise worthwhile clients. For example, the credit disbursements under the Erzurum Rural Development Project in Turkey showed dramatic improvement after 1985, when it began accepting assets created out of loans as collateral instead of land titles.

Timeliness in the delivery of credit is very crucial. The dictum 'credit delayed is credit denied' is applicable nowhere more than in rural credit. Rural borrowers cannot afford to wait indefinitely in uncertainty. The shorter the time lag between application and disbursement, the better for the rural borrowers. In the case of the money lender, who is not circumscribed by externally imposed rules, credit delivery is much quicker. If he makes a mistake, he suffers for it. In credit institutions, where lendings take place through several outlets and where employees work on salaries (which are unaffected by their *bona fide* miscalculations), formal procedures are inevitable. However, it is often possible to streamline these procedures, cutting many avoidable delays. Following are some of the ways in which this could be done.

(*a*) The management should state clearly the loan policies of the bank.

(*b*) Authority for sanctioning loans should be decentralized to lower levels and to regions.

(*c*) Loan officers should be encouraged to take more responsibility for individual loan decisions.

(*d*) Appraisal procedures for smaller loans could be made separate and more simple.

(*e*) Information on borrowers should be collected and stored systematically, if possible through the use of mechanization.

(*f*) Loan appraisal manuals could be prepared consolidating all the instructions on loan approval.

Whether loans should be delivered in cash or in kind would depend upon the individual circumstances. Delivery in kind would be appropriate in areas where arrangements for this are satisfactory. The extent of liaison between the lenders and the supply institutions is a crucial determinant here. When loans are issued in kind, temptations for diverting loan proceeds for consumption would be less, but this would restrict the choice of the borrower in selecting the required material. At times this may also result in delays in procurement. One hundred per cent repayment has been reported under a village seed bank scheme supported by Oxfam in Gujarat, India. These seed banks provided local seed at the time of the planting season and collected the same amount of seed grain at the time of harvest plus 25 per cent extra towards interest. In the province of Punjab in Pakistan where loans to members of co-operatives were given in kind and repaid in kind, recovery was as high as 97 per cent. In other provinces where this procedure was not followed, recovery was around 20 to 40 per cent.

Another, related, issue which is often neglected in credit programmes is the method of dissemination of information on various credit schemes supported by lenders. When the potential clients are widely dispersed, shy of formal lenders, and illiterate, getting information to them is important. Spreading information on credit schemes can go a long way towards stimulating genuine credit demand among rural poor. A successful example of such promotion of credit by using local images and expressions is that of the Banco Agrario del Peru.

Field animators

Field officers are the cutting edge of any rural credit programme. It is their perception, involvement, and efficiency that, to a large extent, decide the quality of the credit. They act as a link between institutions and rural clients by performing a range of functions such as identification of borrowers, preparation of bankable schemes, disbursement of credit, assistance in the productive utilization of credit, collection of repayment, mobilization of savings, etc. A whole range of issues relating to their selection, training, placement, job-evaluation, motivation, rewards, and punishments needs to be tackled effectively to improve the quality of lending. The attitude of persons towards living in rural areas and performing a job amidst rural clients is important when selecting them for the job. If higher academic qualifications are prescribed to improve the quality of personnel, often it may prove to be counter-productive, as they may be unwilling to serve in rural areas. While imparting training to them, the emphasis should be on 'hands-on' training, and on materials and case studies which have relevance to actual field conditions. For example, training centres established by the African Co-operative Savings and Credit Association (ACOSCA) provide basic inputs relating to book-keeping, auditing, community development, leadership, etc. for field level officials. Interestingly, Professor A. F. Laidlaw, who studied training establishments in India during the mid-fifties, made the following remark: 'In my opinion the centres for training junior officers are most important in the whole system and should, therefore, have the best staff and facilities, for the co-operatives in India are going to succeed or fail on the day-to-day work of the junior officers rather than on the administrative work of their superiors.' The effort should be to build a cadre of field agents with the following attributes.

(*a*) An appreciation and sympathy for the problems of small farmers and rural disadvantaged.

(*b*) Familiarity with the social setting and production activities in the farm and non-farm sectors.

(*c*) A basic knowledge of banking, accounting, and financial management.

(*d*) An elementary technical knowledge relating to rural activities.

(*e*) An awareness of the resource potential of the area.

(*f*) Preparedness to move out in the field rather than do a desk job.

In short, the field officer should be able to act as guide, philosopher, and friend to rural clients, and be able to dispense 'counselled credit' rather than the conventional 'supervised credit'. The Twenty-Ninth Report of the Estimates Committee on banking in India (1985–6) suggested practical steps to make work in rural areas for rural bankers less stressful through provision of residential accommodation, educational allowances, and welfare measures. The Committee pointed out that simple exhortation to take up rural banking as a challenge without such supporting services would be fruitless. Rewards for better performance could be either in monetary forms – advance increments, promotions, lump sum payments, prizes, etc. – or in other forms such as merit certificates, club memberships, training opportunities etc. More than that, there should be a clear definition as to what constitutes effective performance, making reward and punishment more objective, which can boost the morale of field workers. Fixing the workload of loan agents should be done scientifically. Too many, as well as too few, loan accounts per loan agent can create problems. To increase their mobility in the field, bank agents should be provided with appropriate transport, a bicycle, motorbike, Jeep, etc.

Similarly, fixation of salary levels for them should be done taking into account remuneration levels of comparable field agents in government machinery. The mobile credit officers in the Agricultural Development Bank of Pakistan (ADBP) operate from branch offices and cover about 25 villages each. They assist borrowers in identifying and preparing investment plans, facilitate loan approval, and also supervise loan use. The ADBP's project appraisal unit helps in improving the quality of appraisal by their agents. Specialists from other disciplines such as soil and water conservation, livestock, etc. support ADBP field agents and small farmer technology unit and rural communication system provide appropriate technical support to its borrowers. In Africa some development banks, e.g. Fonds National de Developpement Rural (FONADER), have utilized the field staff of government agencies, for distribution of inputs and recovery of credit, against a small fee. These banks could reduce their loan administrative costs by this arrangement.

It is worth while to recollect the principles of field staff management adumbrated by Dr Robert Chambers:

Field staff are dispersed and almost invisible. Supervision is difficult. A high degree of motivation, responsibility and initiative are needed if they are to work well. But field workers are presumed to be low calibre and lazy. This view is, however, self-validating. It is partly because they are treated as low calibre and lazy that their performance is poor. By treating them as responsible, by giving them a part in defining work plans for themselves, by giving them satisfying tasks, and by a system of supervision which brings their performance to the notice of their superiors, their behaviour will change for the better. Although complementary reforms in terms of service, promotion prospects, and other personnel matters are desirable, an early improvement can be achieved through the introduction of systems of management procedures designed and tested for specific situations.[5]

Transaction costs

Transaction costs for the lender include all administrative overheads associated with lending: staff salaries, establishment expenses, transportation, bookkeeping, etc. Transaction costs for the borrower include his travel costs, expenses on documentation, and other incidental expenses for borrowing.[6] If he has to forego earnings in the process of waiting for a loan, that too would add to his transaction costs. These costs vary markedly from region to region and also from institution to institution and precise estimates are hard to come by.[6] Reduction in these costs is, however, possible under the following circumstances.

(a)   Just as the small size of loan pushes up average costs, an increase in the number of loans brings it down.[7]

(b)   Innovative lending experiments like group lending, mobile credit officers, etc. can reduce the cost of lending.

(c)   Computerization and mechanization of loan accounts can bring down transaction costs.

(d)   Transaction costs on non-collatered credit would be lower than on collatered credit.

(e)   Decentralization and streamlining of procedures would bring down overall costs for both lenders and borrowers.

(*f*)   When lenders have more information, as in the case of repeat borrowings, the cost of lending would fall.

(*g*)   When savings schemes are operated along with credit schemes, lending costs tend to decline.

Monitoring and evaluation[8]

The monitoring and evaluation system of financing agencies should be able to provide management with timely information on current implementation problems, as also policy guidelines for future lending. Some of the questions to which a monitoring and evaluation system should try to provide answers are:

(*a*)   Who are the recipients of credit?

(*b*)   Did they face any constraints in receiving credit?

(*c*)   What happened to the activities financed?

(*d*)   Did the borrowers repay the loan as stipulated?

(*e*)   What are the major constraints at the lender level, borrower level, and government level? How could they be removed?

(*f*)   What lessons do they provide for future projects?

In sum, it may be stated that the effectiveness of rural lending depends on the quality of loan appraisal and loan approval procedures, commitment of field animators, incidence of transaction costs, and soundness of monitoring and evaluation systems.

CHAPTER 9
Reaching the Rural Disadvantaged

What have we learnt from development?
Development leaves the great bulk of the popu-
lation unaffected.

ARTHUR LEWIS

TO IMPROVE the access of the rural disadvantaged to financial services, many experiments have been tried in developing countries. Co-operatives, rural bank branches, mobile banks, area development projects, and group lending are some of them. The principal factors which influence their access to the formal financial system are proximity, range of services, cultural identification, and participation.

Proximity. When the banking outlets are situated far away from their residences and fields the rural poor find it difficult to forge an effective relationship with them. Financing institutions, on their part, find it difficult to locate offices in remote areas. There may not be adequate business potential to support an office. Considerations of security of cash and other valuables may also dissuade them from going to remote areas. Under such circumstances, mobile credit officers could take banking to the doorstep of the clients. Under the 'one-man village banker scheme' in Pakistan, a resident of the village is appointed as the Banker by the financing institutions, and he is accessible to clients at his residence all through the day. Keeping banking hours and days flexible is another way to improve accessibility. For example, on a weekly market day the branch could remain open from early morning until late evening and it could remain closed on some other days of the week. Such variations should be allowed for individual banking units, depending on local customs and cultures. Another way to improve access is by publicizing credit schemes through illustrative promotional pamphlets using local images and expressions.

Range of services. When the rural poor see that they can depend on the formal agencies for a variety of services, their confidence in them increases. When banks co-ordinate supply of needed inputs like seeds, fertilizers, etc. they become more popular in the rural community. This also happens when credit agents work as effective extension agents explaining to farmers the latest cultivation practices. In India, the Syndicate Bank through its subsidiary Syndicate Agriculture Foundation opened 'farm clinics' adjacent to rural branches to provide extension services to small borrowers. These 'farm clinics', apart from helping the bank to identify prospective poor clients, held stocks of inputs and other materials needed by the rural poor. Borrowers know that these are the services they cannot obtain from the village money lender. Provision of consumption credit and loans to meet emergencies are other essential services needed by the rural poor. As Michael Lipton noted: 'The conclusion, rather, is that credit is a total problem, and that only when formal and informal sources together, and competitively, meet consumption credit needs will small farmers readily demand and apply producer credit'.[1] Availability of savings schemes that synchronize with their small and irregular cash flows can also improve the confidence of the rural poor.

Cultural identification. Often there exists a perceptible cultural gap between formal lenders (especially when they have their origin in the urban environment) and rural borrowers. Bank agents with an educated background may exhibit an attitude of superiority to rural clients. The rural poor may feel uncomfortable with sophisticated bank officers. A borrower feels alienated when the field agents look on him as a dependant to whom some favour is shown. The rural client looks with suspicion on the expert and his advice, although he may outwardly show a subservient attitude towards the expert. From the borrower's point of view, the wisdom accumulated over long years of practical experience is superior to the academic wisdom gained through formal education. Thus, for the field agent with all his theoretical knowledge, the farmer looks 'traditional' while, for the farmer, the field agent appears as 'impractical'. Much can be done to improve their communication, by appropriately orienting the bank agents. They should be prepared to honour the practical wisdom of the borrower and to shed their superiority complex. The message they give should be more in the way of practical demonstration than platitudes. When farmers see that bank agents are prepared to learn from them, it opens up the way for more effective communication between them.[2]

People's participation has now been recognized as an important element in all rural development programmes. In rural credit programmes also, this is now gaining acceptance. For many years, the rural poor saw credit programmes as something alien, launched by a benevolent government. They never viewed these programmes as their own. This was partly because those who conceived these programmes in the past never thought that such participation was really necessary. People's participation in the lending programmes can be encouraged in several ways. Borrowers could be represented in the management of banks. Lenders could meet groups of rural poor periodically to know their problems and preferences. Rural people can also participate in financial intermediation through savings. When the rural community sees the financing agency as their own, they develop some stake in its successful operation. In India a novel experiment known as 'Volunteer Vikas Vahini' has

56

been tried by the National Rural Development Bank, to ensure people's participation in credit programmes. Under this scheme selected borrowers are chosen to spread the messages relating to credit schemes, repayment obligations, etc. (see also Chapter 11, section relating to people's participation).

Group lending

A system of loaning which is now becoming increasingly popular among many lenders across the continents, to improve the access of the rural poor, is group lending.[3] Group credit can be defined as non-individual credit in which credit is given to groups of farmers joined together in some sort of association, co-operative, credit union, user's society, etc., and where such organizations play a role in the securing, management, use, and repayment of such credit. Thus the association acts as an intermediary between the credit granting authority and the ultimate user. Although the experience has been mixed, group lending has the following potentials.[4]

(*a*) Increased accessibility of the rural poor to formal lenders.
(*b*) Availability of scale economies not only in credit but also in providing other related services. For example, operating large-scale equipment individually could be costly, while in a group it could be economical.
(*c*) Reduction in borrower and lender transaction costs.
(*d*) Improved loan recovery. (In the case of the Agricultural Development Bank in Panama, default ratio for December 1985 was 11.9 per cent for groups as against 21.2 per cent for individuals.)
(*e*) Greater generation of personal savings.
(*f*) Provision of a sense of security and self-reliance among participants.
(*g*) Scope for better borrower participation and financial responsibility.
(*h*) Generation of group activities in spheres other than credit.
(*i*) Reduction of corruption by loan agents while dealing with individual borrowers.

Realization of all these advantages would depend on the individual circumstances. However, as a concept, group lending has not been fully accepted in parts of Africa (e.g. Tunisia) and Asia (e.g. Indonesia). If group lending is to succeed, there have to be a number of factors present.[5]

1. The social environment and its characteristics must be conducive to group formation. If people are highly individualistic, group functioning

57

will be difficult. Participation in groups involves sacrificing some individual freedom and benefits. Only when the advantages derived from group membership are substantially more than these costs, do people stick to groups. In cases where people are very poor and group formation is the only way open to them to improve their lot, the group approach succeeds.

2. Homogeneity of membership is another factor. When all the members come from similar social and economic backgrounds, groups become stable. The Brazilian co-operatives formed by Japanese immigrants provide a typical example where cultural homogeneity acted as a powerful unifying force. Similarly, if all the members produce the same commodity the chances of disintegration are comparatively less. When groups consisting of both big and small farmers are formed, they tend to fail due to differing interests. Under the Niger Range and Livestock Project in Central Niger, associations which included a mixture of Twary and ex-slave households did not become fully participative due to status differences.

3. The way groups are organized is an important determinant of their success. Groups with more than ten members generally lose cohesion. When the rules and regulations for group formation and functioning are simple, clear, and well understood by members, it removes many irritants in the course of group operation. Groups hold together better when members attend regular meetings and have a common contributory fund. When members willingly perform honorary services, it brings down group costs. When leaders, secretaries, treasurers, and other office bearers receive training in managing group finance and other activities, the group succeeds better. Another essential condition for group success is the presence of honest and efficient management.

4. Another factor relates to the type of external intervention in group formation. It has been found that when the field agents of the banks are committed and efficient, they can successfully promote groups. Experience in Nepal has substantiated this. Similarly, when individual groups are affiliated into a federation, they become a stronger force.

5. When groups are formed only to receive credit they disintegrate quickly. If, however, a credit function is added to an existing group activity, such groups have better chances of success.[6] Overall, it must be said that group formation is more an art than a science. When governments interfere too much, group initiatives fail. At the same time groups cannot survive without policy support. Thus the strategy dilemma is to provide needed support without too much intervention. In other words, the self-reliance of local groups should be carefully nurtured while providing a protective environment.

Some major weaknesses of group lending have come to the surface of late. Group leaders have been found taking undue advantage of the facilities available to members. Groups consisting of extended family members have failed to meet repayment obligations. In many credit groups in the Philippines there has been almost no peer pressure on members to effect repayment. In Ghana lenders could not enforce joint liability. When several members of the group failed to repay, the lender had to absorb the loss. The defaulters were then dismissed from the group and a new loan was granted to a reconstituted group. Among groups formed within extended families it was found difficult to impose discipline on members who were relations as well. In some cases, members who were prompt in their repayment found it burdensome to own the debts of defaulting fellow-members, and consequently opted out of the group. Little can be accomplished through group credit in countries where there is a highly inequitous land distribution pattern.

Philippe Egger, after studying some of the successful groups, noted:

Whether the groups are formed spontaneously, through the catalytic work of a trained animator, or a motivated bank worker in the field, or even through interaction with other groups, they must reflect the members' own motivation and aspirations. The members must perceive the group as an instrument for furthering their own economic and social interests and enhancing their human dignity. Obtaining credit is only one phase in this process.[7]

Some experiences of rural credit programmes which attempted to reach the rural disadvantaged are given below.

Grameen Bank Project in Bangladesh (GBP) (Currency Taka: Tk)

The Grameen Bank Project in Bangladesh was initiated in August 1976 to provide finance exclusively to landless or near-landless for undertaking a wide variety of farm and non-farm activities. The Grameen Bank was subsequently converted into a public sector specialized credit institution with a paid-up capital of Tk 30 million (40% owned by government, 40% by members, and the balance by two banks). To be eligible for credit a borrower has to satisfy two conditions: he or his family should own less than half an acre of arable land (or assets worth less than one acre); and he should join a bank credit group.

Grameen Bank workers assist in the formation of such borrower groups of about five members each. Six to ten credit groups are federated into a Centre. Each group elects its own Chairman and a Secretary. These chairmen in turn elect a Centre Chief and a Deputy Centre Chief. Loan requests of each member are first scrutinized by the group, then by the Centre Chief and the bank worker. Two members are chosen as first loanees, and if their repayment performance is good loans are provided to others. Loans are given to individual members of the group, but the group stands guarantee for the loans. Loans are available for more than a hundred diverse rural activities such as rural trading, rickshaw pulling, livestock, fisheries, tea vending, etc. Loans are normally given for a year at 16 – 18 % interest and have to be paid back in weekly instalments. Groups meet once a week, when the bank worker collects repayments as well as deposits. The bank worker is the key element and he prepares loan applications for each loanee as also a loan utilization sheet for every loan disbursed. Attendance at weekly meetings is compulsory. Each member contributes one taka weekly and 5% of the loan is added to a Group Fund from which needy members can avail loans for consumption. In addition, members contribute an amount equal to 25% of interest on the loan to an Emergency Fund. This fund is utilized for payment of insurance premium, meeting contingencies like sickness, death, etc. By August 1986 the Grameen Bank was operating 257 branches covering 4491 villages (about 3% of all the villages in Bangladesh) with a membership of 208, 543, of whom 148,284 were women. Total loans disbursed were Tk1300 million. Loan recovery was nearly 100 per cent. Accumulation in the Group Fund and Emergency Fund was Tk88 million and Tk16 million respectively. The following factors contributed to the success of this programme.

(a)   The field workers were well motivated and trained. Rural people developed a lot of faith in them.
(b)   Formation of groups was done very selectively. Before forming a group, members underwent intensive training to familiarize themselves with credit schemes and bank procedures.
(c)   Prospective clients saw bank loans as their last chance for survival due to abject poverty prevalent in the rural areas.
(d)   For the rural poor, groups provided an opportunity for participation as also a sense of security.
(e)   Specific attention was paid to the needs of rural women. Separate female groups were organized by female bank workers.
(f)   The rules for group operation were simple and flexible.
(g)   The project inculcated a habit of savings among the rural poor. The Group Fund and Emergency Fund helped the members to meet several contingencies for which normally institutional loans were inadmissible.
(h)   Above all, the Grameen Bank has a committed leader in Professor Yunus, who managed the whole programme with a great deal of vision. The close field supervision and guidance has, however, meant high lender transaction costs to GBP at around 25%. With a lending rate of 16%, GBP's profits have been declining sharply from

Tk4.2 million during 1984 to Tk0.4 million in 1985. Such deterioration in profitability could inhibit its further expansion.

Peasant Farmers Development Institute in Nicaragua (PROCAMPO)[8]

INVIERNO (the Peasant Farmers Development Institute) was created in May 1975 as an autonomus organization to serve the rural poor by combining credit with other supporting activities like extension, input supply, and marketing. The programme initially focused on a few regions and tried to extend basic services to the rural poor. The areas selected for project services were less than twenty-five kilometres from the zonal office and had a minimum population density, proximity to a serviceable road, and some agricultural potential. Credit was provided through mobile banks at 18% interest. Community leaders were trained about the objectives of the programme. This kind of peoples' participation generated interest in the programme and also helped to schedule services according to the needs of the people. An effective Management Information System was developed to control the field operations in the isolated rural communities. Using computers facilitated quick processing of loan applications. Computerization speeded up the accounting process, and provided timely information on input needs, loans due, etc. Loan application forms were simplified to a two-page document and this facilitated electronic data processing. Loan approval criteria were standardized. As many as 10,000 loan applications could be processed in a week due to standardization and computerization. Borrowers were given a five-year line of credit which, while reducing the transaction costs, increased their sense of security. Repayment schedules were flexible and synchronized with farmer incomes. During good times higher amounts were recovered and during bad times concessions in repayment were given. The project created a trained field agent known as 'Agromoc' who motivated and advised the farmers regarding new agricultural practices. 'Agromoc' was in fact an agronomist with additional training in human relations. He acted as a liaison man with the community on agricultural technology. Overall the system was highly suited to offer small amounts to large numbers of isolated farmers lacking collateral. By June 1978, over 20,000 small loans (average $175) had been disbursed to 8500 small farmers (owning less than two hectares). The repayment rate under the programme was 90 per cent. Although after 1979 the programme was renamed PROCAMPO, much of the contents of the earlier programme were kept intact. This is a unique case where modern data processing facilities were extensively used to reach the rural poor. Its success was mainly due to the following factors.

(a) Credit was provided along with the necessary supporting services, right at the community level.

(b) Computerization facilitated rapid and effective processing of loan applications. This also led to standardization of loan application forms and approval procedures.

(c) Maintenance of one comprehensive account per client and fixing a line of credit reduced the operational costs.

(d) Involvement of local people was ensured through consultations.

(e) An effective cadre of field agents was developed through proper selection and training.

(f) A good management information system enabled the programme to initiate corrective steps promptly.

Group lending in Malawi
(currency Malawi Kwacha: MK)

In Malawi group credit was introduced in 1973 under the Lilongwe Land Development Programme (LLDP), primarily to reduce lending costs. Each credit group consisted of 10–30 members and had a chairman, a treasurer, and a secretary who performed the administrative functions. In view of the prestige associated with these positions, most of them worked in an honorary capacity. Ten per cent of the loans were credited to a security fund, to cover the risk of defaults by individual members of the group. Group formation and disbanding was simple and non-bureaucratic. This flexibility enabled groups to get rid of chronically defaulting members. Short-term loans to members for seed and fertilizer were isued in kind through the government agency responsible for their supplies. Interest on group loans was 10%, as against 15% on individual loans. By 1979 over 1200 credit groups were functioning in the LLDP project area serving about 28,400 farmers. This constituted nearly 50 per cent of LLDP's loan portfolio. Loans disbursed to groups had increased from Mk21,000 during 1973–4 to Mk805,000 by 1978–9. Overall, these credit groups increased the access of small farmers to credit, reduced transaction costs, and improved crop production. Although there was not much difference between repayment records of groups and individuals, at around 100 per cent, the efforts needed for collection in the case of the latter were much higher. The following factors contributed to the success of the project.

(a) Group credit in Malawi was preceded by group input supply. Earlier, the State trading monopoly had encouraged formation of groups, by offering a discount on bulk purchase of fertilizer.

(b) Groups were formed along traditional kinship and communal lines which ensured loyalty and discipline.

(c)   A relatively equitable distribution of land holdings (around 1.5 ha) and a socio-cultural pattern congenial for group formation contributed to group cohesiveness. Groups were in fact formed at the initiative of the farmers with minimum government interference.

(d)   The agricultural development strategy in Malawi emphasized the need for extension and other support services as a pre-condition for credit expansion.

(e)   The interest concession of 5 per cent for group loans when compared with individual loans acted as an incentive for group formation.

(f)   Groups were simple in operation and membership was flexible. The project administration gave specialized training in self-accounting to the groups.

(g)   The services of the managers and other office bearers were practically free.

Farmers' Service Societies in India
(currency Rupees: Rs)

The National Commission on Agriculture in 1971 recommended formation of Farmers' Service Societies (FSS) in India to improve the access of small farmers to credit. FSS were to extend a full package of services to farmers along with credit. They were in effect a modified version of the existing village co-operative credit societies, which were not very successful in meeting the credit needs of small farmers. Unlike these village co-operatives, each FSS covered a wider geographical area (a 'block' covering several villages) and a population of around 10,000. Although FSS were to serve all types of farmers in its area of operation, management was to be represented by small farmers to the extent of 66%. Started in 1973–4 with 30 FSS, by the end of June 1978 there were 1577 FSS with a membership of 3.3 million. Of this around 0.6 million had borrowed loans to the extent of Rs690 million by 1977–8. Unpaid loans as of that date were Rs262 million. As against a paid-up capital of Rs173 million, their deposits were just Rs69 million. A study by the Reserve Bank of India in 1980 found that most of the FSS were no different from other village co-operatives. The FSS experiment illustrates that even innovative schemes to extend credit to the rural poor will not work if the system in which they are allowed to operate has weak spots. The following were the major deficiencies in the functioning of FSS.[9]

(a)   Many FSS had an overlapping jurisdiction with the existing village co-operatives. Since both were co-operatives operating at the village level, this created much confusion.

(*b*)   Very few FSS could reach a business turnover of Rs1 million, which was necessary to maintain viability in operations.

(*c*)   Many FSS did not have trained technical staff and consequently they could not provide the necessary supporting services. This was both cause and effect of poor loan business.

(*d*)   Like all other village co-operatives, FSS also could not mobilize much savings or help farmers in their marketing.

(*e*)   Despite mandates restricting big farmers' role in management, they continued to dominate the FSS and also to pre-exempt much of its credit.

Group lending in the Dominican Republic
(currency Dominican Peso: DP)

The Dominican Development Foundation (DDF) was organized in 1966 as a non-profit organization to promote the social and economic development of the rural poor. DDF was the first agency anywhere in the world to experiment with group lending and was unique in the sense that it blended into its activities the interests of private, corporate, government, and donor agencies. The number of groups financed annually by DDF steadily increased from 42 (2081 members) in 1966–7 to 393 (6923 members) in 1973–4. After reaching this peak point, the number of groups started declining steeply and by 1978–9 there were only 124 active groups (2590 members). However, over all these years DDF's loan portfolio steadily increased from DP0.1 million in 1966–7 to DP6.3 million in 1978–9 indicating a steep increase in the per capita group loan (average loan size per group was DP2802 in 1966–7 and DP12926 in 1978–9). The size of the groups varied from ten to one hundred individuals and they had no legal basis. Once the groups were formed, a DDF co-ordinator arranged a meeting to explain DDF's programmes. Loans were provided to the groups, for specified activities like rice production, by the DDF through banks located in the vicinity of the groups. The secretary of the group kept records of loan transactions of members. Members were jointly liable for loan repayment, although this was not legally enforceable. Over the years many groups disbanded, some even without repaying their loans. Some groups were recombined by DDF into larger groups. While the reasons for group failure varied, the following reasons were most common.

(*a*)   When groups were organized only for the purpose of availing a loan, they did not last long. Groups which had been together for some time prior to getting a DDF loan and which had been realizing other 'group goods' exhibited better cohesion and permanence.

(*b*)   Groups organized among recent migrants who had not yet developed social ties disintegrated soon.

64

(*c*)　The nature of joint liability for loan repayment was not clear to members. This weakened group solidarity.

(*d*)　Increased loan defaults and reduced external assistance caused resource constraints at DDF. There was also deterioration in the quality of loan services provided by DDF. Delayed loans from DDF necessitated temporary borrowings from informal markets. DDF started losing its credibility and borrowers did not attach much importance to keeping a good credit rating with DDF.

(*e*)　As against the lender transaction costs of forming and supervising groups, which was estimated at about 20 per cent of outstanding loans, interest charged by DDF was 10%. DDF tried to reduce consequent losses, particularly when its funds position started deteriorating, by reconstituting smaller groups into bigger groups.

(*f*)　Groups that contributed a significant part of the resources needed for the project performed better than those groups which had relied substantially on bank loans to meet the project cost.

It is clear from this case that a number of factors contribute to the success of group lending. When groups are organized primarily to avail institutional loans without any other cementing force, they are not likely to hold together for long.

CHAPTER 10
Delinquencies and Default Problems

If you go to Carey Street, you will see a lot of
people with long faces. They are creditors. You
may also see one man beautifully dressed, wear-
ing a gardenia in his buttonhole and smiling
happily. He is a debtor.

GEOFFREY HOWARD

'As WOULD be expected, delinquency rates are a good indicator of
project success. Unsuccessful projects had delinquency rates that ranged
from 10–75 per cent, with most falling between 25–50 per cent. The successful projects had delinquency rates from 0–15 per cent with most
below 5 per cent. The rates in partially successful projects were around
20 per cent. Although comprehensive default data are not available, it
appears that successful projects had rates of 2 to 3 per cent.' This was
the conclusion of the USAID evaluation study[1] which reviewed 50 rural
credit projects funded by AID between 1973 and 1985 around the
developing world.

The presence of delinquencies and defaults indicates the extent of
profitability of the activities undertaken with the help of credit; the
capacity and will to repay – as affected by such things as flood, drought
or illness as well as by 'repayment ethics' prevalent in the borrower
community; and the effectiveness of the financing agency in loan
administration.

It has often been found difficult to draw a line of demarcation between
delinquencies and defaults. While delinquencies indicate delay in repayments, defaults denote non-payment, and the former if unchecked leads
to the latter.

Non-repayment of loans has several undesirable consequences. It
gradually destabilizes the credit system. When defaulters are big farmers
the system becomes unjust inasmuch as they are subsidized by small
farmers who repay promptly. In fact the AID *Spring Review* (1973),
found that in many countries, particularly in Colombia, Bolivia,
Bangladesh, Costa Rica, Ethiopia, and Sri Lanka, it was the big farmers
who defaulted more. Costs of administration of overdue loans are high[2]
and defaults push up lending costs without any corresponding increase
in loan turnover. Defaults reduce the resource base for further lending,
weaken staff morale, and affect the borrower's confidence.

There are marked variations in the methodology of computing
defaults, as shown below. Consequently measuring and comparing
defaults in different credit programmes have become increasingly
difficult.

(*a*) Distinction between delinquencies and defaults is drawn in different ways. This makes it often difficult to classify overdue loans period-wise.

(*b*) Default rates are calculated in different ways. Some relate the unpaid amounts to loans actually fallen due, while others relate it to total outstanding portfolio. Unpaid loans are denoted as a percentage of loans disbursed during the year in some other institutions.

(*c*) Treatment of interest on loans also markedly varies from institution to institution. Some institutions do not calculate interest on loans long overdue. Some appropriate the repayment first to outstanding interest and only the balance to the principal.

(*d*) The method of writing-off of bad debts also differs considerably. Some keep accounts receivable for indefinite periods, while some others transfer them to blocked accounts after a specified period.

(*e*) To present better results to donors, some window-dress the recovery performance by refinancing unpaid loans, thus making them current through book adjustments. Conversely when individual loan officers accept rewards and permit late repayment or rollovers, it increases apparent incidence of delinquency.

(*f*) In many institutions the correct arrear position is not known due to defects in accounting. Undue delays in postings, use of suspense and sundries, keeping consolidated entries for different activities, delayed publishing of accounts, etc. make it difficult to know the extent of default.

The World Bank identified three general reasons for overdues:[3] failure of farmers to use borrowed funds for productive purposes, failure of investments undertaken, and refusal to repay despite realization of additional incomes. Nimal Sanderatne, after a comprehensive survey of defaults in Sri Lanka, identified six factors which contributed to defaults:[4]

(*a*) defects in farm production systems;

(*b*) variability in incomes caused by fortuitous, seasonal, or unforeseen factors;

(*c*) defects and inadequacies in the organization disbursing credit;

(*d*) attitudinal conditions not conducive to repayment;

(*e*) misallocation of borrowed funds;

(*f*) miscellaneous reasons such as illness, death, etc.

Remi Adyemo identified the principal cause of loan defaults in Kwara State, Nigeria, as loss of production due to natural calamities.[5] He found that educated borrowers and land owners repaid loans more promptly than uneducated and tenant borrowers. A study in India found that defaults were by and large wilful and mostly large borrowers were responsible for them.[6]

Causes of delinquencies and defaults could be classified as relating to three levels: borrower level, financing institution level, and economy level.[7]

Causes at borrower level

1. Loan officers often thrust a loan on an unwilling borrower in order to complete loan quotas or targets. An unwilling borrower turns out to be an inefficient producer and a defaulter.

2. Borrowers who deliberately divert loans to non-essential consumption find it difficult to meet repayment commitments on time.

3. Investments fail to generate sufficient incomes due to improper technical advice, absence of supporting services, inadequate marketing, etc. Investments also fail due to unforseen causes like floods, drought, etc. In both cases repayment would be affected.

4. When borrowers have liabilities towards informal lenders, they get precedence over institutional lenders.

5. Contingencies at the borrower household like death, sickness, etc. affect repayment performance. Formal institutions which do not extend consumption and emergency loans are liable to have higher default rates.

6. If the borrowers are at a very low level of subsistence, any additional income generated through loan-supported activities is likely to be appropriated for basic needs.

7. Borrowers would like to delay repayment when the real rate of interest is low.

8. Absence of incentives for prompt repayment, and of penalties for delayed repayment, could promote defaults.

9. Borrowers who are politically powerful or those who have the right contacts, tend to delay repayments.

Causes at financing institution level

1. Defective procedures for loan appraisal in the financing institutions could lead to the financing of bad projects and consequent defaults.

2. Quality of loan officers, their mobility in the field, and their capacity to judge borrowers as also the incentive packages available to them affect repayment performance. When loan officers are assessed more on the basis of compliance with lending targets than with recovery

68

performance, it could lead to bad loans. When responsibility for lending and recovery are vested with separate officials in a credit agency, recovery tends to decline.

3. Fixing of inappropriate repayment schedules and lack of flexibility often result in defaults. Similarly, when the procedure for repayment is cumbersome borrowers tend to delay repayments.

4. Defaults have a 'spread effect' particularly in the marginal cases. When lenders show reluctance to enforce sanctions against conspicuous defaulters, defaults tend to increase through a process of imitation.

5. When borrowers use various services of the lender, like money transfer, safe deposit, savings scheme, etc., they come in contact with the lender more frequently. On the other hand, when institutions are simply lending windows their contacts with borrowers become limited. Consequently their ability to collect repayments also becomes restricted.

6. Financing institutions which educate farmers on the nature of credit schemes, responsibility of borrowers, etc. can expect better repayments. Similarly, innovative lending schemes like 'group lending' can improve repayment.

7. A sound accounting and management information system is essential for better repayments. Only when the lender knows how much is due from whom, and when the amount is due will he be in a position to follow it up. Absence of sound book-keeping has been the major cause of defaults in many institutions.

8. Defaults tend to soar when loan portfolios show signs of shrinking (this itself may be due to defaults) as farmers would be reluctant to repay when they were not sure of getting new loans.

Causes at economy level

1. When overall government policies, particularly those relating to pricing of inputs and outputs, marketing, land tenure arrangements, etc., discriminate against the rural sector, they make rural activities unprofitable, leading to defaults. Both borrowers and lenders are helpless in this environment.

2. Faulty monetary and fiscal policies of governments could result in high inflationary conditions. Borrowers tend to delay repayments in such a situation to take advantage of the fall in value of currency.

3. Interest rate policies of governments have a vital role in the promotion of repayments. When the real rate is excessively low, borrowing and consumption will be much more profitable than saving and repayment.

4. Excessive government intervention in the day-to-day administration of financial institutions could result in bad loans.

5. Some national governments indemnify financial institutions for the losses arising out of poor loan collection. This could weaken the latter's efforts to collect loans.

6. Wholesale remission of farmers' debts, stalling of recovery proceedings of institutions against wilful defaulters, public announcements protecting defaulters, etc. are often done on political considerations. Under these circumstances, borrowers expect an implied government protection in the case of non-repayment. Farmers soon start demanding government intervention and delay repayment lest they miss the concessions on the anvil. Government policy in relation to debt collection has a vital role in promoting 'repayment ethics' among institutional borrowers.

7. Often governments have weak local machinery for planning and executing development programmes. This could result in lack of co-ordination between credit supported activities and other support services, causing defaults.

8. Calamities like droughts, floods, market glut, etc. could affect farmer incomes and consequently their repayment.

Looking for remedies[8]

The types of remedies needed to contain defaults would depend upon the causes. It is, therefore, necessary first to assess which of these factors have contributed to loan defaults. This analysis itself often becomes difficult as more visible but not necessarily important causes tend to conceal the vital issues. What is effective in one country or situation may be inappropriate in another country or situation. Even one group of borrowers would not react the same way under all conditions.

Delinquencies are the initial symptoms that something has gone wrong somewhere. Experience shows that financing agencies tend to neglect these initial symptoms and consequently intervention at a later stage, when the disease has taken deeper root, becomes less effective. Many a borrower slides in the scale gradually to become a hard-core defaulter. During the initial stages he may postpone repayment for minor reasons etc. then, when he finds that he can indeed avoid repayment without much sanction, he joins the 'defaulters gang'. One important point often underestimated regarding default is its proliferation by imitation. Recovery of loans is indeed a hard task, particularly for formal lending agencies which are governed by set rules and where loan officers work on fixed salaries which are usually unrelated to recovery. Sometimes they have to use hard policies like disposing of assets, enforcing other legal remedies, etc. to collect debts and these could alienate borrowers. At other times they have to use 'soft policies' like a polite reminder, friendly admonition, etc. to ensure that borrowers repay and at the same time continue to identify with the institution. It is a difficult and complex task to arrive at an appropriate mix of hard and soft tactics. The most important determinant of repayment however, seems to be the borrowers' 'will to repay'. It is this 'will to repay' that has to be nurtured using different tactics. When borrowers identify themselves with the lenders, this 'will to repay' becomes much stronger than otherwise.

A high rate of recovery in the People's Republic of China (in 1981 the Agricultural Bank of China and the rural credit co-operatives granted loans of 274 billion yuan and recovered 267 billion yuan, constituting 97 per cent recovery) has been achieved by the adoption of an integrated approach covering all aspects of agricultural production from supply of inputs to marketing. Similarly, high recovery in the Republic of Korea was due to increase in farmer incomes under government price support programmes for rice, and close loan supervision by banks. The Bangkok Bank, a private commercial bank in Thailand, had operated a small farmer credit programme since 1963 with higher rates of recovery than several other commercial banks. This was because the bank assessed each farmer's holding with respect to soil capability, cropping pattern, costs, yields, and family expenses before arriving at his credit eligibility. On the other hand, high loan defaults in Sri Lanka were attributable to undue government intervention to push agricultural loans. The large defaults in the Philippines were on account of inadequate government support to agriculture and consequent low profitability of farming.

Gordon Donald has noted: 'While focusing attention on defaulters we must remember that they are in the minority in almost all the credit programmes. Credit programmes could hardly remain in existence if they were not. In stating generalized reasons for default such as poverty, social distance, lack of economic incentive to repay, etc., we are speaking of forces which are also at work for the repaying majority of farmers – in other words, they are forces that are not universally victorious. They represent problems to tackle, but not impenetrable barriers to credit programmes. It is true, of course, that institutional credit reaches a small fraction of farmers in most developing countries, so that if more borrowers were reached, the pro-default forces may find more scope. Still, the experience with farmers who have had institutional loans provides evidence that the prospect is not hopeless.'[9] Experiences of some of the rural credit programmes in loan recovery are discussed below.

Rural credit programme in Jamaica
(currency Jamaican Dollar: J$)

There was a substantial increase in the volume of institutional credit for agriculture in Jamaica during the 1970s: loans outstanding increased from J$25 million in 1970 to J$168 million in 1978. Agricultural loans by the Jamaican Development Bank (JDB) increased during third period from J$0.5 million (2 per cent of total institutional lending for agriculture) to J$27 million (16 per cent). This increase in JDB lending was mainly due to the support provided to it by the World Bank, CDB, and IADB. JDB mainly financed large farmers for capital intensive activities like tractors, plantation orchards, etc. Loan arrears of JDB, which were 2.2 per cent of total loans outstanding in 1974, increased to 19.6 per cent by 1978. The following factors contributed to defaults in JDB.

(a) Due to high inflation, real interest rate was negative to the extent of minus 18 per cent.
(b) Overall economic recession in the economy.
(c) Loan appraisal procedures of JDB were deficient in many ways.
(d) Account keeping at JDB was faulty and consequently precise arrears rates could not be worked out.
(e) There was no machinery within JDB for effective and timely collection of loans.

Loan arrears in three other small farmer credit programmes, Agricultural Credit Board (ACB), Crop Lien Program (CLP), and the Self Supporting Farmers Development Program (SSFDP), in Jamaica were equally bad. ACB's arrears in 1978 were 39 per cent of its loan outstanding. Deficiencies in accounting, management, loan approval and collection were the factors which contributed to its high loan arrears. CLP was a financial failure with 6 per cent recovery. Launched in 1977, it disbursed J$9.5 million to 30,000 small farmers in less than one and half years of operation. Officials implementing the programme had no accountability and there were no effective sanctions against default. CLP loans were seen more as grants than loans. SSFDP had a relatively low rate of arrears at 18 per cent of loans outstanding. Close monitoring of loans and a highly decentralized system of operations contributed to better collections in SSFDP. This, however, substantially increased its operational costs as compared with other small farmer credit programmes. Overall, the Jamaican experience indicates that when loans are disbursed under government pressure without observing banking norms, the results can be disastrous. It also shows that the cost of supervision of small loans can be substantially high and that, although such close supervision could reduce defaults, in the end it may not necessarily be more cost-effective than a high default, non-supervised system.

Agricultural co-operatives in The Republic of Korea
(Currency Waun: W)

During the early 1960s, two-thirds of farm households in Korea were depending on informal lenders for their credit needs. The proportion of institutional borrowings to total borrowings of farm households at 34 per cent in 1964 increased to 75 per cent by 1982, while 95 per cent of institutional borrowings during 1982 was from agricultural co-operatives as shown below.

	(Million W)
Total farm household borrowings	1.382
Institutional borrowings	1.035
Borrowings from co-operatives	0.984

The ratio of farm household overdue loans which was at 12.8 per cent in 1976 declined to 9.5 per cent by 1982. If we exclude overdue loans up to one year, this percentage would drop to 3 per cent. Good recovery by agricultural co-operatives was on account of the following reasons.

(*a*)   The average farm household incomes had gone up from US$140 in 1962 to US$5963 in 1982. This steep rise in incomes increased the repaying capacity of borrowers.

(*b*)   Farmers were able to borrow in time and in required quantity due to the flexible lending procedure followed by co-operatives.

(*c*)   Government policies supported efficient land use and improved marketing.

(*d*)   Co-operatives had an efficient loan approval, supervision, and collection machinery. Farmers were sent notices one month before due date of loans.

(*e*)   Hardships of farmers due to natural calamities like cyclone, floods, drought, etc. were taken care of through an emergency fund created for the purpose.

(*f*)   Moral persuasion by bank agents was highly effective in cases of default, as the community did not look with favour upon defaults to co-operatives. Thus socio-cultural factors particularly the 'Confucian work ethic' played an important role in promoting good recovery.

Medium-term credit programme of Organisme Regional de
Dévelopement *(ORD) in Burkina Faso* (currency Francs: FCFA)

Medium-term credits to small farmers were extended by Eastern ORD in Burkina Faso under a USAID-supported Integrated Rural

Development Programme. A study was conducted in October 1978 to find out, among other things, the reasons for large loan defaults under the programme.[10] The analysis among 869 borrowers showed that 37 per cent of the cases were due to the fault of the borrowers, another 37 per cent due to the fault of the lending institution, and the balance of 26 per cent due to natural calamities. There was confusion regarding the measurement of default rates. Administrators of the programme chose to use the default definition most convenient to them. For example, when delinquent loans were expressed as a percentage of total outstanding loans, it worked out to just 2 per cent (FCFA0.71 million delinquent loans as a percentage of FCFA51.9 million outstanding at 1978), whereas the same as a percentage of the amounts actually due increased to 31 per cent (FCFA0.71 million as a percentage of FCFA2.3 million due). When it was necessary to show high recovery rates the former was chosen and in other cases the latter.

The following factors contributed to defaults:

(*a*)   Borrowers felt no obligation to repay ORD, which in their view was a part of the government. They reasoned that the government had anyway collected taxes from them.

(*b*)   ORD's appraisal system was deficient in many ways. It did not properly work out the debt capacity of the borrowers and loans were often disbursed untimely.

(*c*)   ORD agents went to collect loan repayments without warning. When borrowers had surplus cash after selling their produce, ORD agents did not approach them. The man who went to collect repayment was different from the man who made the loans.

(*d*)   Many borrowers were unaware of the terms and conditions of the loans. They had given gifts to the loan agents expecting them not to recover the loans.

(*e*)   Low crop yields, ill health, and other family contingencies had also contributed to defaults.

Ironically, some of these very same borrowers were prompt in repaying the money lenders. This was because they wanted to get further loans from him, the money lender was located near and accepted repayments in kind at the time of harvest, and he was strict in enforcing repayment obligations; also, any failure led to the disgrace of the borrower's family.

The study concluded that it was possible to keep defaults within limits even in drought-prone areas like the Sahel. The conventional excuses of bad weather and recalcitrant farmers were used more as a cover for the shortcomings of the financing agency. ORD experience showed that a lot can be done by the financing agency to improve collection. More careful loan screening, incentive systems to credit agents, strict enforcements of repayment obligations, asset insurance, arrangements to meet contingencies, etc. could significantly improve loan collections, if the financing agency were willing to try them seriously.

Rural credit programme in Sri Lanka
(currency Rupees: Rs)

Due to a government directive to step up agricultural loans, there was a sudden jump in formal institutional credit in Sri Lanka during 1977–8. The Central Bank of Sri Lanka (on behalf of the government) guaranteed these loans to the extent of 75 per cent. Agricultural lending by two major banks, the People's Bank and the Bank of Ceylon, increased from Rs180.70 million in 1976–7 to Rs527.60 million in 1977–8. Such compulsion from the government encouraged banks to lend rather indiscriminately. Recovery level at the end of 1977–8 declined to 26.2 per cent of loans outstanding as against 73 per cent during 1972–3. Due to this alarming rise in defaults, government withdrew the guarantee cover. Recoveries somewhat improved from 1978–9 when bankers became prudent in their lending. The other factors which contributed to 1977–8 defaults were natural calamities, provision of more loans than necessary, and poorly motivated field agents.

Earlier, during 1971, the Central Bank of Ceylon had conducted a survey of 841 defaulters to co-operatives, covering loans availed during 1967–70. This survey identified the following reasons for defaults.

(*a*) One-third of the defaulters reported crop failure as the reason for non-payment. However, the statistics on crop yields indicated a much lower rate of failure, implyng that farmers used this reason as a pretext for non-repayment.
(*b*) Some of the farmers defaulted due to receipt of low incomes. This in turn was due to non-availability of adequate support services like irrigation, inputs, etc.
(*c*) Many farmers had reckoned loans as grants not to be repaid.
(*d*) 9 per cent of the defaulters mentioned that they did not repay as no one had asked for it. 8 per cent did not repay as they had no trust in the loan agents.
(*e*) Political interference, malpractices of government officials, and contingencies like illness or death were some of the other reasons for non-repayment.

Policy support to ensure viability of the farming, stabilization arrangements in case of crop failures, and proper loan appraisal and follow-up were seen as measures to improve loan recoveries.

Lendings by commercial banks in Costa Rica
(currency Colone)

During the period 1969–74, the delinquency rates of four commercial banks, which provided virtually all formal agricultural credit in Costa Rica, ranged between 30 and 38 per cent of loans outstanding. If temporary overdues up to 90 days were excluded, these rates dropped to around 10 per cent during all these years. Recovery rates were better for agricultural loans when compared with non-agricultural loans. Also in Costa Rica, the lowest default rate was found in small farmer loans. (To qualify as a small farmer, a borrower should have a net income of less than 25,000 colones and total bank loans of less than 100,000 colones.)

However, this apparent good performance concealed some discriminations and distortions in credit allocation. Small farmer loans carried a lower interest rate of 8%. This, combined with a rate of inflation ranging from 5% in 1969 to 20% in 1974, had made real interest rate negative: consequently demand for loans was much in excess of supply. Unlike in many other countries, low interest rates did not promote defaults in Costa Rica; rather they encouraged repayment. What prompted farmers to repay was the prospect of getting still more cheap credit on repayment of the earlier loan. Unlike in many other countries, bank employees in Costa Rica were better paid than civil servants. Their benefits and promotions were linked to the bank profits and thus they had a stake in ensuring higher profitability. Consequently it was in the interests of branch managers to keep costs down and defaults to a minimum. Decentralization of loan approval powers enabled them to use their discretion while selecting clients and to keep information costs to the minimum. In this process loans were given only to the best borrowers with prior success in farming and good repayment record. Genuine new borrowers and loans for new crops got completely excluded, as gathering information about new crops was considered costly and lending to new borrowers risky. Overall, this experience showed that low defaults *per se* were not an indication of a sound credit allocation. They could mean stringent loan rationing against many needy small farmers and promotion of less productive activities.

As pointed out by Robert C. Vogel: 'The stated objective of low interest rates on agricultural loans, especially to small farmers, is to promote development activities and to benefit disadvantaged borrowers. However, as shown above, these deserving borrowers are in fact more severely limited in access to bank credit than other borrowers. Moreover, low delinquency rates do not provide evidence that bank loans are used to finance productive activities in the agricultural sector. Negative real interest rates, such as existed in Costa Rica for bank agricultural loans in 1973 and 1974, mean that borrowers can undertake projects with negative real rates of return and still generate enough income to repay bank loans.'[11]

The Masagana-99 Programme in The Philippines
(currency Peso: P)

Masagana-99 (M–99), which began in 1973, was the first attempt by the Philippines government under a supervised credit scheme. The programme's main aim was self-sufficiency in rice production through doubling rice yield, for which it offered an integrated package consisting of inputs, credit, technical assistance, and market support. By 1974 credit under M-99 peaked at P1.13 billion to more than 530,000 borrowers, roughly one-third of all rice farmers in the country. Although yields and production increased substantially, credit declined over the years. By 1982–3 loans granted under the programme were around P220 million. High defaults had disqualified most borrowers and the participating banks from getting fresh credit. The following were the major reasons for defaults under M-99.[12] (see also Chapter 11 section relating to M-99)

(*a*)   Due to regressive pricing policy, farmers who participated in the programme could not profit from rice farming. They reacted by not repaying institutional loans.

(*b*)   Many farmers had believed that bank loans came from government and were not to be repaid.

(*c*)   Level of education of the borrowers influenced repayment behaviour: 59.5 per cent of defaulters had at most only elementary schooling, while 54 per cent of prompt repayers had been to high school or college.

(*d*)   Only 41 per cent of the borrowers had actually used the loans for farming operations. The rest, who had used it for food purchase, medical care, education, etc., could not repay.

(*e*)   Those who did not have a marketable surplus could not repay the loan. Natural calamities were one reason for poor yields and limited surplus.

(*f*)   90 per cent of farmers who became ineligible for formal credit due to defaults, resorted to borrowing from the money lender and this led to sharp increases in village money lending. This experience showed the importance of appropriate pricing policies in creating a healthy rural credit system. Repayments are markedly influenced by the operational efficiency and financial strength of lenders which in turn is determined by the extent of defaults.

CHAPTER 11
The Profitable Deployment of Credit

Banking is the surest, safest, easiest business I have ever known. If you are not actually stupid or dishonest it is hard not to make money from banking.

GEORGE MOORE

As MENTIONED earlier, credit can be expected to perform its legitimate function only when there are profitable activities in the rural economy. A typical case is that of the Green Revolution in India in the 1960s. Dwarf wheat varieties developed by CYMMIT, Mexico, and new rice varieties developed by IRRI, Philippines, were well suited to conditions in several parts of India. Together with large amounts of fertilizer, reliable water supplies, and power, they represented a powerful technical package to increase yield and cropping intensity many times. However, without these supports, high yielding strains were not very much better than traditional seeds. Farmers who had their own resources could get access to water, power, and fertilizer and adopt the new varieties quickly. Prompted by the success of these early adopters, many other farmers in the area too wanted to practise the new package, but could not do so for want of financial resources. To them bank finance indeed provided the missing link with which they could invest in wells, pumpsets, tractors, etc. USAID's recent evaluation of credit projects reinforced this conclusion. 'In all of the successful projects, supporting services were appropriate. In all of the failures, they were not. In projects that failed, technology and supporting services did not exist or were woefully inadequate, with the following specific problems:

– Expected yields were well below anticipated levels
– Improved seed, fertilizer and extension services were not available in a timely manner
– Crop prices and marketing arrangements did not meet expectations.[1]

Technology and extension

A given technology represents a particular combination of factors of production. Under 'traditional technology' in farming, land, labour, seed, fertilizer, water, and machine power have been combined in a particular way, and that combination has proved to be useful in an area over a long period of use. A 'new technology' implies the introduction of changes in this combination by adding a new factor, by dropping an existing one, or by changing them in one way or the other. A new technology need not necessarily come from scientific invention. Any practice which has not been previously used by farmers in a given area can be termed new. While some changes may necessitate considerable investment, many others may not. The important issues while changing the existing technology are:

– Is the new technology more profitable than the existing one?
– How much more risky is it than the existing one?
– Can it be practised by farmers under their field conditions?
– Would the extension agents be able to bring it to the doorstep of the farmer?

In other words, unless the new technology is more profitable, less risky, and accessible, it would be futile to push it to the farmers. The technology package which produces a higher yield is not necessarily welcome unless it also reduces the perceived risk of the farmer. Given their low level of income and the vagaries of weather, their fear of trying something new is reasonable, although often not appreciated by extension workers.

Similarly, farmers would trust the extension worker only if the latter has sufficient practical experience regarding the new technology. In fact evidence from programmes like M-99 in the Philippines (see Chapter 10) shows that if the technology is sufficiently profitable, it will be adopted even without much credit support. The Minya Agricultural Development Project in Egypt is a good example of developing appropriate technology packages. Thanks to government encouragement, research centres developed viable technology packages for bean cultivation. When this was combined with good extension, small farmers adopted the new technology much faster than anticipated. The technical unit of the Grameen Bank in Bangladesh known as Studies, Innovation, Development and Experimentation Unit (SIDE) is another example where a multi-disciplinary staff investigate a number of new technologies and disseminate them among bank members.

Markets, storage, and transport

Technology could help in increasing production, but unless the surplus produce is marketed and converted into cash, borrowers will not be able to meet their repayment obligations. In fact, even without new technology, new markets in themselves could generate a lot of activities supported by credit. Under the Grameen Bank scheme in Bangladesh and the Integrated Rural Development Programme in India, a range of activities in the tertiary sector could be supported by credit due to the availability of markets for their products.

Marketing encompasses a host of other activities like storage, transportation, organization, etc. In most developing countries marketing is carried out in widely scattered places by large numbers of people. Marketing of rural produce is an extremely complex phenomenon. Existing knowledge as to what happens in this long 'marketing chain', why it happens, and how to influence it in favour of smaller rural producers is rather scanty. Farm products have high weight/value ratios and are more liable to seasonal and annual fluctuations. Similarly, storage of most farm products is more costly per unit value. Storage is also risky as they decay fast. Given the high weight/value ratio of farm products and the small-scale nature of the transport, the cost of moving farm products is higher than for other products. All these factors make the marketing of rural products extremely complex. Although better storage and transport facilities could improve access to markets and help realize better incomes, often farmers may not be willing to incur the costs and risks associated with such improvements. Financing institutions can lend money to build storage capacities so that farmers need not sell their produce in distress to middlemen. Similarly, credit for marketing could help farmers to wait for better prices. Governments could also help these activities through public investment. This may benefit other members of society as well, when it results in reduced price fluctuations, reliable supplies, etc. Government can extend support to marketing by assuring minimum support prices. It can organize marketing through government marketing boards. Such efforts can succeed only when government's overall planning to match outputs with demand is done on a scientific basis. Often governments are unable to anticipate production and demand at a given level of price during a given period. Consequently, increase in productivity and production could lead to market gluts. This is what happened in the case of potatoes in Costa Rica and Peru during the 1980s.

Pricing policy

Pricing policy relating to inputs and outputs is crucial to the profitability of rural activities. Policies of cheap food for urban consumers, high taxes on agricultural inputs, etc. could make agricultural production unremunerative. In fact, marketing issues cannot be viewed in isolation from price policies. In Jamaica, under an Integrated Rural Development Programme, despite a low interest rate of 6% on institutional credit, farmers refused to take loans as government price controls had made farming unprofitable. In Zambia, commodity prices set by the government allowed low profit margins, and farmers availed credit (later to be defaulted) only to supplement their profitability.[2] In many other African countries faulty government policies made investment in agriculture unprofitable. Michael Lipton noted: 'In Kenya and most other LDC's, if demand for agricultural credit is low, it is largely because urban bias keeps down the prices of the extra goods that credit-financed farm investments can produce ... As with rural education, so with rural credit; a policy to supply more, without a policy to render its utilization relatively more rewarding would do little or nothing to remedy the present unfair and ineffective situation.'[3] On the other hand, in countries like Japan, the Republic of Korea, etc. government price policy ensured the profitability of farming and consequently credit programmes in these countries had a better record of success. Even in Africa, in the case of Zimbabwe, maize production dramatically increased from 1981, when government raised the maize price and abolished price controls. This price support, along with the marketing support provided by the Zimbabwe Grain Marketing Board, contributed to the success of the new small-scale credit scheme. In the early 1970s the government of Indonesia began a credit programme through Bank Rakyat Indonesia (BRI) to support rice production and it was thought that rice production had increased due to sufficient availability of credit (at around 12%) from BRI. But after the mid-seventies, rice production continued to increase despite a sharp decline in credit supplied by BRI. This was because a price rise of about 30 per cent above import prices stipulated by government for rice, was seen as a great incentive by farmers. All these prove that pricing policy has a marked influence on rural activities.

Supply of inputs and other materials

Timely supply of inputs is important, especially in agriculture which depends on the vagaries of nature. Inputs are of two types: current inputs and capital inputs. Current inputs include seeds, fertilizer, and other supplies, while capital inputs include farm machinery, pumpsets, etc. Financing agencies can give loans in cash to borrowers who can on their own acquire these supplies or they can instruct suppliers to deliver these items directly to farmers against their loans. Delivery in kind relieves farmers of the need to handle cash transactions on their own, and when financing agencies procure them in bulk, there may be price advantages to the borrower. But delivery in kind restricts the choice of the borrower and when institutional supplies are undependable, farmers will face more problems. On the other hand, when loans are given in cash, farmers may be tempted to use it for their more pressing consumption needs or at times even for unproductive use. Loans in cash may add to the borrower transaction costs, as the farmer will have to go to both the bank and the supplier. Decisions as to whether credit should be given in kind or in cash would depend on factors like level of awareness

81

of farmers, network of the supply agency, etc. In both cases, financing agencies should ensure that adequate supplies of inputs financed are available. For example, in Bangladesh, the Krishi Bank encountered problems in the distribution of hand tubewells. The dealers appointed by the Bangladesh Agricultural Development Corporation responsible for input and equipment supply were reluctant to supply them to farmers with the existing low commission admissible to them.[4] When government corporations undertake supplies, problems could arise due to bureaucratic delays.

Infrastructure and other supporting activities

No economic activity can take place without adequate infrastructure and other supporting services – roads, transport, communications, power, water, etc. If they are absent and not likely to be available in the foreseeable future, it would be futile to pump credit into those areas. Credit cannot undo these deficiencies and many credit programmes operating in such an environment meet with failure, so much so that some rural credit experts maintain that all these facets of rural development should be part of a single programme. Without feeder roads farmers would find it difficult to get their produce to the market. Without proper transport, reaching the bank branch would involve additional cost and time, thus increasing the borrower's transaction costs. With poor communication facilities, access to information becomes limited. Without reliable power, supply pumps will remain idle. If the land tenure system is defective, tenant farmers will not have incentives to commit borrowed funds to production. In the Philippines, rural credit dramatically increased during the mid-1970s when, almost overnight, tenancy was abolished by Presidential decree in 1973. Training of farmers is another essential supporting activity. So also is the insurance cover available to the borrowers. The Caja Agraria Colombia includes a life insurance policy in its loan contracts. For a premium of one per cent added to the interest rate, the loan balance is repaid by the insurer if the borrower dies. In Mexico, the estimated risk of 13 per cent in crop production, is borne half by farmers and half by the State. Arrangements to protect the lenders from losses arising from small loans have also been in operation in several developing countries. The Agricultural Credit Guarantee Scheme Fund (ACGSF) in Nigeria is a good example. Established in 1977, ACGSF guarantees 75 per cent of principal and interest up to N50,000 in the case of individual loans and N1 million in the case of loans granted to co-operatives, by commercial banks in the agricultural sector. The cost of ACGSF is shared between the Central Bank (60%) and the Government (40%). Combining credit with insurance has however proved to be very costly and without substantial

82

government subsidies such schemes have not been attractive to either lenders or borrowers.

Co-ordination

Responsibility for much of the infrastructure and supporting activities is spread among different ministries and departments of the government. Often they work in isolation, one not knowing what the other has programmed. Overlapping functions and lack of co-ordination are more a rule than an exception in many developing countries. Moreover, in a typical developing country resources are scarce and allocation among different regions and sectors has always been problematic. Under these circumstances three types of co-ordination are required: between the various government development departments; between the various financing agencies; and between financing agencies and development departments.

Such co-ordination can be effected through formal machinery established at the national, regional, and local levels. Problems could be sorted out at periodic meetings of these committees constituted for the purpose. The Technical Board for Agricultural Credit in the Philippines and Agricultural Credit Advisory Committee of State Bank of Pakistan are both good examples of how co-ordination among different programmes and agencies can be achieved through a top-level advisory machinery. At the field level, co-ordination can be better facilitated if the bank worker can effectively liaise with other line agencies. Co-ordination can be achieved by drawing credit programmes within an overall development programme. However, if all activities are managed by a single agency in the effort to ensure co-ordination, the credit function is likely to be neglected. Mils-Mopti in Mali is a typical example of failure due to poor co-ordination. The project had several components – supply of credit for agriculture, provision of inputs to small farmers, assistance in the repair and improvement of roads, improvement of village wells, training of blacksmiths, etc. Since it covered too many activities, it became complex and could not succeed in ensuring the necessary co-ordination. In Egypt a network of village banks has been in operation since 1977. In each village bank there is a Farm Management Team comprising the bank manager, agricultural extension officer, financial analyst, accountant, veterinarian, representative of the input supply organization, and some leading farmers. This team extends integrated services to the farmers. This kind of field level co-ordination enables farmers to select suitable technology, assess their financial needs, and procure inputs in time. In India preparation of District Credit Plans have been found useful in ensuring co-ordination among different agencies.

83

People's participation

Credit institutions which operate without local participation have limited chances of success. Such people's participation has to be genuine and broad-based. Any external intervention should activate local participation rather than replace it. Co-operatives in India are an example of undue State intervention which dampened people's participation. In several developing countries, financing agencies serve as a one-way link between governments/aid agencies and rural people. Rural people view them as alien institutions to be taken advantage of while the going is good.

People's participation can be promoted in several ways. When financing agencies trust their clients and solve their genuine financial difficulties, people start developing confidence in the formal system. Savings mobilization, innovative lending experiments, earmarking of seats on the management, and frequent consultation with the borrowers could promote people's genuine participation.

In summary, it can be said that a host of factors – technology, extension, markets, price policy, storage, transport, input supply, infrastructure, co-ordination, participation, etc. – determine the profitability of credit supported activities. Many of these, however, lie beyond the scope and control of credit institutions and this makes lending for rural activities an extremely challenging, often underestimated, task. A comprehensive institutional credit survey in India came to this conclusion.

It has been clear that credit can hardly be separated from several factors and considerations which together form one background ... They comprised a whole set of conditions in which production and activities connected with production were carried on. There was the important question of land tenures and tenancies ... the provision of irrigation, supply of seed, manure, etc., the introduction of better technological methods and the availability of the implements needed to supply those methods ... Then there were the stages which followed production such as processing, storage, transport, and marketing, in each of which the agriculturist was vitally concerned. Thus there was a whole range of economic activity to be taken into account along with credit, because of an association so intimate as to present in effect one organic problem for which lines of solution had to be investigated.[6]

Some of the rural credit programmes dealing with these issues are discussed below.

Masagana-99 (M-99) rice cultivation programme in The Philippines

As mentioned earlier, M-99 was an integrated rice development programme started in the Philippines in 1973 and covering a whole range of activities from technical extension, supply of inputs, credit delivery, development of irrigation, etc. Supply dealers and consumers reaped much of the benefit of the programme. The farmers who participated in the programme could realize only limited benefits, primarily due to defective government pricing policies as shown below.[6]

(*a*)   By 1981, the cost of production of rice had increased by 160 per cent (1974 base) due to escalation in fertilizer and fuel prices, and increase in wage rates. As against this steep rise in input costs, productivity during the period increased only by about 50 per cent from 1.9 tonnes of paddy to 2.8 tonnes.

(*b*)   The rate of inflation had reduced the real farm gate price of paddy further. Real prices in 1982 were only 60 per cent of 1972 prices.

(*c*)   While the ceiling price was enforced strictly, the floor price was operated rather flexibly by the government, only as a guide at the time of procurement operations. Also, the floor price was pegged to the 1972 price level, thus denying farmers any income from further productivity gains.

(*d*)   The retail price ceiling relative to the cost of importing rice has been very much lower in some years since 1973. This benefited consumers at the expense of producers. In 1975, the gross margin between ceiling and floor prices became thin and traders procured from farmers at prices lower than the support price.

In short, under the M-99 programme, participating farmers suffered the most from regressive pricing policy. They reacted by not repaying the institutional credit which in effect became a capital subsidy to them. Defaults affected the viability of credit institutions and made them ineligible to borrow further. Overall, this experience shows that even when production objectives are achieved, credit programmes could fail if not supported by appropriate price policies.

Co-operative de Crédit Mutuel (CCM) in Cameroon (currency Francs: CFAF)

CCM was started in mid-1950 as a pilot experiment to provide credit to selected coffee growers. The scheme was operated by the Banque Camerounaise de Développement (BCD) through government agricultural extension workers. Each CCM was a sort of co-operative of 7–30 members. Members could borrow ten times the capital collected by them and deposited in the bank. CCM was initially confined to coffee growing regions but later on expanded to other regions. The progress of CCM over the years is shown below.

	(amounts in thousands of CFAF)	
	1954–5	1961–2
Number of CCMs	1	2364
Number of loans	29	12535
Amount of loans during the year	7125	128406
Cumulative Total of loans	7125	948601

In 1965 BCD had to stop the programme when the arrears were beyond 32 per cent, amounting to 235 million CFAF. There was no way of getting back these amounts from the borrowers. The following factors were responsible for the failure of the CCM experiment:

(*a*)   The scheme did not provide for participation by the members. They viewed it as something imposed from outside to be taken advantage of.

(*b*)   The concept of 'Unlimited Joint Liability' was not suitable to the social circumstances prevailing in the region.

(*c*)   BCD was a government bank without any experience with small farmers. It relied on government extension workers who were themselves unfamiliar with credit operations. Also there was no co-ordination among various administrative services including co-operative departments.

(*d*)   The reward system for extension workers was defective. They received a premium as a proportion of loans disbursed to CCMs. This led to artificial inflating of credit demand and indiscriminate loaning, even indicating fictitious borrowers' names.

(*e*)   Under pressure, BCD agreed to finance construction of houses under the programme. Thus credit was extended to activities which did not directly increase the productive capacity of the borrowers.

(*f*)   The system was allowed to expand too quickly without observing the impact the initial CCMs had made on borrowers.

Magbosi Integrated Agricultural Development Project, Sierra Leone

Under the Magbosi IADP project, it was anticipated that a new technological package would increase the rice yield from about 0.70 to 1.50 tonnes per hectare. As against this projected yield, the actual yield was only 0.9 tonnes per hectare. This reduction in yields upset the profitability calculations relating to farm investments. The appropriateness of the technological packages and the expected increase in yields should have been more systematically studied.

86

On the marketing side, the project had assumed that the high price spread between project area farm-gate price of rice and those prevailing in the urban market of Freetown would continue to prevail. This did not happen and, due to rice imports, the price at Freetown fell considerably. Also during this period, farmers' production costs of rice increased, thus cutting their profitability both ways. Experience of this project indicates the following:

(a)   While assuming increase in yields, what is important is not what is technologically feasible under laboratory conditions, but what is possible for farmers to achieve under their field conditions.

(b)   In the absence of proper extension the gap between the laboratory and the land would continue.

(c)   While making assumptions relating to prices at which outputs can be marketed, one has to be very cautious.

(d)   Viability of farm investments greatly depends upon the cost of investment in relation to input–output price margins.

District Credit Plans in India

A District Credit Plan (DCP), prepared for each district in India, is a mechanism to ensure co-ordination among different financing agencies on the one hand and between financing agencies and the government/ other development agencies on the other. A credit plan covering a district is based on the district development plan and the former sub-serves the object of the latter. The DCP is prepared by a task force consisting of a district planning official and representatives of various banks operating in the district. One of the banks in the district is designated as the 'Lead Bank' (LB) for the district. The LB functions as the overall catalyst, co-ordinator, and consortium leader for all credit-supported rural activities in the district. The DCP, prepared by the task force headed by the LB, is formally approved by a District Consultative Committee where senior banking and government officials are represented. The DCP indicates scheme-wise and area-wise break down of activities to be financed by different banks. These allocations are based on the availability of infrastructural support and natural resource endowments in a given area. The DCP also indicates the scale of finance for each activity identified and included under the plans. Banks make a commitment to implement their share and plan their own overall financial and manpower resources accordingly. The District Consultative Committee, through the LB, monitors the implementation of the DCP, identifies shortfall, and removes constraints in implementation. Despite several operational problems, DCP has been found to be a useful mechanism for identifying potentially viable projects and for ensuring a flow of credit in a co-ordinated way.[7]

CHAPTER 12
Informal Financial Systems

A village is fit to live in only when there is a money lender from whom to borrow at need, a physician to treat in illness, a Brahmin priest to minister to the soul and a stream that does not dry up in summer.

INDIAN SAYING

THE INFORMAL capital markets in developing countries consist of two segments, the non-commercial and the commercial. Loans extended by friends or relatives, mostly without interest, constitute the non-commercial segment. In the commercial segment a range of people like input dealers, crop buyers, landlords, professional money lenders, etc. operate. These agencies function outside the banking systems, and are neither regulated nor effectively monitored by any central authority. In most developing countries informal sources still meet 50–80 per cent of the credit needs of rural people. Governments have been hostile to informal lenders and viewed them as exploiters of helpless peasants. Despite this, money lenders have survived almost everywhere, implying their financial viability, adaptability to rural conditions, and most of all acceptance by rural clients. Ironically, rural people attach more importance to securing a good credit rating with money lenders than with formal lenders. Informal financial systems also operate in rural areas for mobilization of savings. They are generally known as Rotating Savings and Credit Associations (ROSCA) and have been discussed in Chapter 7.

The advantages of money lenders in extending credit to rural people were listed by a comprehensive rural credit survey in India.[1]

(*a*)   There is little that escapes his eye in the circumstances of his debtors or of those who may one day be his debtors. This local feel keeps him in good stead at the time of loan transaction.

(*b*)   He has different kinds and degrees of hold on those to whom he chooses to lend. Least important of all for him is the possibility of having recourse to the law and almost as unimportant is the possibility of acquiring his debtor's property.

(*c*)   It does not follow that he will invoke the forces of compulsion the moment payment has become due. This is a matter on which, being unfettered by institutional codes, he can be as rigid or as elastic as realism dictates.

(*d*)   Having, in the light of all possibilities, decided on whether and how much he is going to lend and on what terms, he is free to follow as flexible a procedure as he likes in regard to the actual operation of lending.

(*e*)   He is able to hand over the money promptly in order that some expenditure which brooks no delay may be helped at once, without having to obtain anybody else's sanction or authorization.

Participants at the Symposium on Rural Credit organized by the Asian Productivity Organization in December 1982 felt that informal credit was more readily accessible to borrowers than formal credit, that the terms were flexible, and this enabled even small farmers (who were ineligible for credit from institutional agencies) to obtain loans, and that they had higher recovery rates than formal lenders. Surveys conducted for the USAID *Spring Review* in Colombia, Mexico, and Chile recorded the following observations by rural people on the money lenders:[2]

'He does not delay, he just says sign this note and take the money . . . all in the same day.'

'Even though I must pay more interest, he gives me more time to pay.'

'They have more confidence in the small farmers.'

'The bank is an all day trip from my farm while he is just down the road.'

'He will buy my crop at harvest time but the bank won't.'

A survey in Chile found that 64 per cent of informal borrowers had received the loan the same day and the rest from two to seven days afterwards. For a formal lender the minimum was a week, the maximum ranging between few weeks to a month.[3]

The positive factors of money lender credit from the point of view of rural borrowers can be summarized as follows.[4]

Proximity. Money lenders reside close to borrowers' homes or to the trading centres frequented by them. Meeting a money lender does not involve either a long journey or a waiting-in period.

Comfortable atmosphere. Minimal protocol, use of borrower's language or dialect, rural style of dress and manners, etc. make the borrowers feel at ease with him.

Quick credit. Money is passed on to the borrowers within hours or minutes of their request. There is hardly any loan application or processing formalities and collateral is not obligatory.

All-time access. Unfettered by rules and procedures, a money lender is available for business at any time of the day and night. For rural people who face emergencies, and who cannot plan borrowings in advance, this offers an extremely convenient mechanism.

Freedom of deployment. A money lender is not really concerned with the purpose for which his borrower uses the loan, so long as he is confident of getting his money back. This gives a lot of freedom to the borrower in using the borrowed funds.

Repayment flexibility. There is flexibility not only in borrowing but also in meeting repayment obligations. Borrowers are free to repay in small amounts at their convenience. In emergencies, repayment holidays can be availed without any formality.

Lower transaction costs. Because of the informality, transaction costs for both the lender and the borrower are the barest minimum. For the lender, there are little if any overhead costs for real estate, written records are minimal, and cost of supervision almost negligible. So also for the borrower, who has to spend little on documentation and other formalities.

These advantages of the informal sector have made them almost indispensable, particularly to small farmers. It is interesting to recall the observations of Pascual C. Dimagiba, a leasehold farmer from Santa Rosa, Nueya Elija, Philippines, who participated in the APO Seminar (1982):

'I am probably expressing a common experience among us farmers in Central Luzon, and very likely elsewhere in the country, when I emphasize that, in general, (i) we farmers are able to obtain loans from non-institutional sources with relative ease, (ii) it is a common tendency among us farmers to treat institutional loans as government doleouts and, consequently, make no special efforts to repay them, and (iii) more of us farmers are likely willing to avail ourselves of institutional loans (and perhaps improve repayments) if the red tape that goes with these loans were reduced to the minimum even when the rate of interest may be raised from present levels.' One AID *Spring Review* field survey in Chile found that over 60 per cent of institutional borrowers were land-owners owning more than five hectares of land. They had more than seven years of formal education, and were using modern machinery for farming. In contrast, over 60 per cent of borrowers from the informal sector were landless farmers. They had no more than primary education and were farming with traditional equipment.

Credit from the informal sector, although easily available, is not an unmixed blessing. The following are the drawbacks of money lender credit.

High interest rates. Although average interest rate charged by the money lender is around 40–50 per cent, there are cases when these rates go well beyond 100 per cent. Often these rates are camouflaged when interest is calculated for shorter time intervals. There are many other subtle ways through which the money lender exploits and intimidates the borrower. Collecting produce at reduced prices, insisting on free labour on his farms, etc. are some of them.

Consumption credit. Most of the informal credit is short-term for meeting consumption expenses like food purchase, medical assistance, ceremonies, etc. Often the money lender encourages unproductive ceremonial expenses and thereby keeps the small farmer in perpetual debt and poverty. Seldom do money lenders provide term loans for investment purposes.

Credit without supporting services. The money lender is not interested in achieving the national objectives of increased food production or poverty eradication. He is least bothered to ensure the increased productivity of the borrower. Thus, unlike the formal lenders, the money lender is neither interested in nor capable of ensuring support services to farmers from other agencies concerned with extension, input supply, marketing, etc.

Absence of banking services. The money lender's capital comes from his own savings. He is not interested in collecting the savings of his clients and improving their resource base. Also, he is unable to offer any other banking service – transfer of money, safe custody, etc. – to his clients.

There is considerable difference of opinion as to whether money lenders enjoy monopoly profits in their lending operations. Many, including governments, feel that the money lender extracts large profits by virtue of his monopolistic position. Others believe that he is a victim of unfair prejudice and that his income just covers the costs and risks associated with rural lending. A study by Barbara Harris in Southern India[5] found informal market money complementing formal loans. There was no exploitative relationship between borrowers and lenders in the informal market. In fact interest rates on informal loans between 12 and 25 per cent were found to be less than the return from trading in agricultural commodities. The lending rate in the informal sector had remained relatively low due to competition among informal lenders. Although interest rate on formal loans was around 13 per cent, inefficient loan administration, lengthy application procedures, untimely credit, inflexibility of repayment, need for collateral, bribes, etc. had made the effective cost of formal loans almost equal to that of informal loans. Another study of informal credit systems in Malaysia noted: 'It does appear at least as far as the survey area is concerned, that there is little evidence of monopolistic-monopsonistic exploitation by informal lenders. Although informal lenders still provide a substantially larger proportion of loanable funds than formal lenders, the survey data indicates that the rural interest rate is primarily made up by the cost of capital, risk and administrative costs and not by monopoly profits.'[6] Table 2 shows the cost structure and lending rates of lenders in the informal sector in the area.

Table 2
(Percentages)

Lender in the informal sector	Opportunity costs	Average administrative costs	Risk premium	Average lending costs	Average nominal interest rate charged
Pawn shop	7	3	2.64	12.64	14.07
Shop keeper	7	3	2.64	12.64	16.38
Money lender	7	3	11.4	21.4	27.44
Rice miller	7	3	5.3	15.3	11.74
Relatives	7	2	5.4	14.4	4.62
Friends	7	2	5.4	14.4	6.84

According to Professor Lipton[7] the high interest rates of money lenders reflect, not necessarily monopoly, but also the following facts. There are many small loans and borrowers, raising the lender's cost curve relating to average cost per $ loaned to total sum loaned; there are not many lenders, so each operates above the minimum of his cost curve; lending has high opportunity costs; and default rates are high.

For better or worse, informal lenders will continue to operate in rural areas, and it would be unwise not to recognize their contribution to rural development. What is really important is to see how best the formal financial system can be improved to serve the rural clientele, side by side with money lenders. At the United Nations Symposium on the Mobilization of Personal Savings in Developing Countries, held in Yaounde in December 1984, it was generally agreed that the informal agencies had greater cost effectiveness than formal agencies. The Symposium recommended that links between these two sectors should be promoted so that rural lending could be more effective. Formal lenders can try to introduce the flexibilities of money lenders, to the extent they would be feasible within an institutional mechanism. When formal institutions provide effective competition to money lenders, it could improve the bargaining power of the rural clientele against the latter. It is also necessary to study closely the performance of money lenders, their costs, resources, efficiency, etc. Such studies would help to demystify some of the myths associated with informal rural lending. It could also contribute to greater transparency in these markets to the advantage of borrowers. Ways of linking formal and informal markets may be thought of.[8] In selected cases, the informal systems could be used as agents of formal systems. Such models for linkage are being developed in some African countries, particularly in the Ivory Coast, Togo, and Nigeria. A positive attitude towards rural money lenders could yield better results for the rural borrower than any legislative repression of money lenders. In fact experience, particularly from India and Sri Lanka, has shown that such repressive measures could only make money lender credit more stringent to the needy rural borrowers. Thus often such measures can be self-defeating. Two programmes relating to informal lending are discussed below.

Production Input Credit Scheme of the Agricultural Bank of Malaysia (Bank Pertanian Malaysia, BPM) (Currency Malaysian Dollars: M$)

The Bank Pertanian, established in 1969, started operating from February 1970 an input credit scheme in selected rice growing areas of West Malaysia. Under this scheme, short-term production loans for inputs were disbursed through coupons which could be encashed by farmers with suppliers. Part of this programme was operated by the bank through a network of intermediary institutions called Local Credit Centres (LCCs). These LCCs were operated both by private agencies (merchants, rice millers, licensed paddy buyers, shopkeepers, etc.) and public agencies (co-operatives, farmers' organizations, etc.). The balance of the input programme was operated directly by BPM through its own branches.

The LCC was responsible for processing loan applications and determining the loan size and input requirements. In addition the LCC disbursed, supervised, and collected the loans. To cover the risks and administrative costs a commission of around 3 per cent was admissible to the LCC out of the interest rate of 4.25 per cent payable by the borrower for a season of about six months. Most of the loans were issued on unsecured basis due to the complications involved in executing land mortgages. The credit disbursed under this scheme increased from M$58,000 in 1970 (for 431 farmers) to M$4.5 million (for 16,885 farmers) by 1974.

The major problems and lessons under this arrangement were:

(*a*) LCCs organized by private agencies had a high rate of credit utilization and a better repayment record than LCCs organized by public agencies. The former could quickly disburse credit without much paperwork as most borrowers were their existing customers. Their intimate knowledge of local conditions helped them to screen loan applications efficiently.

(*b*) In September 1973 the BPM reduced the lending rates from about 9% per season to 4.25% per season.[9] This was found not adequate to cover the lending costs of LCCs.

(*c*) Partly due to reduced profitability, a sufficient number of LCCs did not come forward to join the programme. Consequently, BPM had to operate a large part of the programme directly through its branches.

(*d*) Overall, large farmers were the beneficiaries of credit from LCCs. Despite these problems, LCC experience shows that integrating informal lenders with the formal system is an economical way to extend credit to rural producers.

Loan transaction costs of the money lender – Bolivian case (currency Bolivian Peso: BP)

The Bolivian Agricultural Bank (BAB) was operating since 1975 a small farmer credit programme in the upper valley of Cochabamba. The comparative position of loans extended by money lenders in the area and BAB is given in Table 3.[10]

Table 3

	Money Lender	BAB
Length of loan	3 months	60 months
Loan size	BP 9,600	BP 73,900
Annual Interest Rate	48%	13%
Lender transaction costs	very low	very high
Borrower Transaction Costs		
(a) out-of-pocket costs	BP 76	BP 1,895
(b) time costs	BP 11	BP 824
	BP 87	BP 2,719
(of this, costs in application phase)	BP 79	BP 1,393

These differences in costs and terms of lending between formal and informal lenders had the following implications.

(*a*) BAB, in its anxiety to lower transaction costs, disbursed mainly medium-and long-term loans. Hence small farmers who required short-term production loans approached the money lender.

(*b*) Similarly BAB's high borrowing threshold (i.e. application phase costs) at BP1393 prompted farmers who needed smaller loans to go to money lenders whose threshold level was BP79.

(*c*) Money lenders could operate at much lower lender transaction costs than BAB. This was because the money lender was located near to his client, knew him well, and consequently there was no need for him to collect additional information on borrowers.

(*d*) BAB's operations had no effect on the business of the money lenders. This was because each one catered to different financial needs, i.e. one on small loans of shorter duration, the other on big loans of longer duration.

(*e*) Borrower transaction costs were least in the case of the money lender. The borrower had to visit him only once or twice, as the

94

money lender himself had the power to take decisions on loans. This experience shows that beyond a point formal lenders like BAB would not be able to reduce lender transaction costs. For the purpose of internal control and financial accountability, public institutions will necessarily have to maintain paperwork and documentation. When banks are operating through several branches, standardization of procedures and formats is inevitable. BAB's case shows that when lender transaction costs are high, banks would try to pass on part of it to borrowers, especially when lending rates do not cover all these costs. Such shifting of costs is done partly as rationing mechanism and partly as a cost saving device. Whatever may be the lender's rationale for doing it, one could conclude from this that small farmers in such cases would gravitate to informal lenders where their borrowing costs are the least although interest rates are high.

CHAPTER 13
Creating Self-Sustaining Rural Financial Institutions

*One could enlist three stages of development in
the history of scientific thought: ability to deal
with problems of simplicity, ability to deal with
problems of disorganized complexity and ability
to deal with problems or organized complexity.*

WARREN WEAVER

DIFFERENT aspects of rural financial intermediation have been discussed
in the foregoing chapters. Better appreciation of these problems and
issues should eventually lead to the promotion of self-sustaining rural
financial institutions in developing countries. This is the linchpin of any
successful rural credit programme, as in an atmosphere of floundering
and weak financial institutions neither the borrower nor the lender can
benefit. The four yardsticks of successful rural financial institutions are
viability, self-sufficiency, accessibility, and efficiency. These factors are
closely interrelated. What is important is the achievement of an
optimum combination, rather than one objective at the expense of the
other.

Viability

Institutions should be able to meet their administrative costs without
recourse to external subsidies and assistance on a perpetual basis.
External assistance may be resorted to, if necessary, only during the
start-up time of new institutions. Such temporary support should be
structured in such a way as to help the institution to earn reasonable
profits in due course and create its own reserves. The overall financial
environment in which an institution operates has a great influence on its
profitability. Lending rate, borrowing rate, loan turnover, and transaction costs are the four principal factors which determine institutional
profitability. As discussed earlier, fixation of lending rates for agriculture and rural development is a complex issue.[1] From the financing
institution's point of view the following factors are relevant while fixing
the lending rates:

(a) It should be *sufficiently high* to cover costs of lending, to provide
for bad debts, and to make a reasonable profit.
(b) It should be *positive*, so that the institution's equity capital is
protected.
(c) It should be *flexible*, so as to maintain its efficiency as the
allocator of scarce capital among competing objectives.

96

(*d*)   It should be *progressive*, in the sense that incidence of interest on large loans is more than on smaller loans.

(*e*)   It should be *differentiated*, so that interest on long-term loans is higher than on short-term loans.

How to arrive at an optimum mix of these rather conflicting objectives depends on individual country circumstances. However, the evidence collected during the course of writing this book indicated that any rate of lending below 18 per cent (real) is not likely to meet most of these objectives (see Annex I). This is because a financial institution is like any other business; if it tries to sell low and buy high, it will soon go bankrupt or have to seek external subsidies to keep afloat.

Interest rates paid on borrowings would depend on the source of borrowings. Funds from donors and central banks are likely to be cheaper than other sources but external sources are often unreliable, and depending exclusively on the profits available from such funding may not be prudent. Mobilizing local savings, although slightly more expensive, has other advantages (see Chapter 7), particularly its reliability.

One important aspect relating to viability which is often overlooked is the fact that profitability is more a function of volume of business than of the absolute margin between borrowing and lending rates. While smaller loans may be costlier to administer, the incidence of cost can be reduced by increasing the volume. Higher margin with lower volume would be less profitable than lower margin with higher business, in view of the large fixed cost component of transaction costs. Increase in turnover would be possible through a sort of 'saturation lending' covering larger number of clients under all categories – small farmers, medium farmers, large farmers, and other non-farm activities – within the geographical area of the branch. Thus, although preference could be accorded to weaker sections, confining lending exclusively to this group would be self-defeating.

Self-sufficiency

Self-sufficiency in resources is possible through reducing defaults, mobilizing savings, and guarding against decapitalization by inflation. Some argue that when financing agencies have access to cheaper funds from donor agencies, they should not be asked to mobilize deposits which are costlier. They imply that even when rural savings are plentiful, the cost of collecting and serving such small deposits together with interest payable would make it uneconomical. Recent evidence, however, shows that the so-called cheap donor funds are not really that cheap, nor the overall deposit costs that high.[2] The cost complementarities that financial intermediaries can attain through the provision of multiple services suggest that economies of scope can be more important than economies of scale. For example, in Honduras the lending costs of commercial banks which depended on internal sources of funds were substantially lower than that of the Agricultural Development Bank which depended more on donor funds.

Prompt loan recovery is another side of self-sufficiency (see Chapter 10). Institutions which combine lending with deposit mobilization, become more familiar with the applicants' cash flow, savings habits, and wealth. This facilitates better loan appraisal decisions and consequently reduces defaults. It also brings down loan administration costs.

Inflation can gradually decapitalize financing institutions. Under inflationary conditions it would be profitable for borrowers to delay repayments. Periodic adjustment of nominal rates or indexing of loans could be done under particularly hyper-inflationary circumstances. In selected cases repayment in kind may be tried. Under a project in Bolivia, farmers received a variety of inputs and all were valued in terms of number of potatoes. If the loan was valued at, say, 100 potatoes, borrowers were asked to repay 120 potatoes or the equivalent. In Chile, under a livestock project, farmers were given loans that were expressed in terms of number of cows. Repayment was effected by delivering cattle to lender. In a project in Niger, farmers received from the lender 1 kg of millet seed and had to repay 2 kg of produce at harvest.

Accessibility

It would be self-defeating if viability and self-sufficiency were achieved by confining lendings to big farmers. In that case the new rural credit programmes would in no way be different from the traditional commercial banks.[3] Hence, accessibility to the rural disadvantaged is an important criterion by which to judge a credit programme. Factors which improve accessibility to the poor have been discussed earlier (see Chapter 9). Shifting the emphasis from collateral to profitability of investment activities supported by credit can go a long way in increasing the access of the rural poor to institutional credit. When small borrowers see that they can get all the necessary supporting services for bank-financed investment activities, their confidence in the banking system increases. Similarly, when bank branches are spread widely in the rural areas, it will encourage small farmers to borrow from institutional sources. Decentralization of loan approval powers, effective interaction by loan agents, flexible lending procedures, lower borrower transaction costs, savings facilities, etc. encourage the rural poor to participate in financial intermediation. Simply earmarking funds to weaker sections, without correcting these distortions, would only result in the pre-emption of credit by privileged people.

Efficiency

As we have seen (Chapter 1), the process of financial intermediation is an answer to the transaction costs involved in (a) direct contact between surplus and deficit units, (b) management of reserves, and (c) the reduction of risks. Although financial intermediation reduces overall transaction costs in the economy, it does not completely eliminate them. In fact the process of intermediation itself brings with it some new costs. Effective intermediation in essence implies overall reduction in such transaction costs. This would be possible only by maintaining a high level of efficiency. No business venture can hope to become self-sustaining without maintaining a high efficiency level and this rule is more applicable to a financial organization. For this, the first prerequisite is a sound manpower planning system covering selection, training, placement, job evaluation, rewards, and punishments. Streamlining of procedures by cutting unnecessary documentation and tiers can improve efficiency. When procedures are codified and responsibilities clear, it smoothens the operations. A good management information system can provide management with information necessary to initiate corrective steps at the right time. Similarly a sound book-keeping and accounting system can improve efficiency. Many institutions find it difficult to assess how much is due from whom and for how long. Often their financial ratios are not really reflective of their true financial position. Computerization and mechanization can be of great help in these areas. Fixing a reasonable number of deposits or loan accounts per officer, assessing the profitability of each operating unit separately, periodic visits to them by senior officials, etc. can improve performance. Financial institutions should fix an ideal level of administrative costs for lending as well as for mobilizing savings. (See Annex II.) They should endeavour to reach this level gradually over a period of time by cutting unnecessary expenses and procedures. An internal committee can be constituted to review periodically the progress in this regard.

Financial institutions should try to achieve all these four objectives of viability, self-sufficiency, accessibility, and efficiency simultaneously. A summary chart showing the impact of various measures on these objectives is given in Annex III. In fact, in view of their close interrelationship, it is often difficult to know whether one objective has been achieved at the expense of another.[4] There are, of course, several external factors which influence achievement of these objectives over which financing institutions have no control. As Gordon Donald has noted:'The objectives or goals of small farmer credit programs and the concerns about their performance, seem to fall into three broad categories. One has to do with the economic efficiency of the activities financed by credit; a second with the ability of a program to serve a hitherto neglected portion of the rural population; and the third with the financial viability of the institutions through which funds are administered. The three can be referred to as the pursuit of efficiency, equity, and institutional viability.'[5]

Some of the rural credit experiments where these issues surfaced are discussed below.

Lending costs in Honduras (Currency Lempiras: LPs)

A comparative study of the lending costs of an agricultural development bank (ADB) and a private commercial bank (PCB) in Honduras was made in 1981.[6] Although there were several private commercial banks and government-owned development banks in Honduras, these two selected banks together accounted for half of formal loans made for agriculture during 1981. Agricultural loans accounted for 75 per cent of the ADB's portfolio and 14 per cent of the PCB's. After studying the income statements of a large representative sample of branches, the following conclusions could be drawn.

(*a*)   The average lending costs (LPs1748) per loan made by PCB was seven times that of ADB (LPs260). However, as the average size of loan of PCB was 22 times that of ADB, loan transaction cost of PCB was only 2.5 per cent as against 8.4 per cent in the case of ADB.

(*b*)   Lending costs of ADB were 77 per cent of overall costs, while lending costs of PCB were only 33 per cent of overall costs. This was because 60 per cent of ADB's funds had come from external sources (and 40 per cent from deposits) while in the case of PCB only 7.1 per cent came from external sources (and 91 per cent from deposits). For ADB deposit mobilization cost was 23% of total costs as against 67% in the case of PCB.

(*c*)   More than 75% of PCB lending costs were incurred at the branch level as against 43% in case of ADB. Such a centralization in operations in ADB was due to its large-scale dependence on external borrowings.

(*d*)   ADB had much more severe problems of loan recovery than PCB. PCB had spent more on loan evaluation – 45 per cent of total lending costs as against 16 per cent in the case of ADB.

(*e*)   In the case of PCB, lending costs in respect of loans made from donor funds was as high as 7.8% of the value of the loans, whereas lending costs of loans made from own funds was only 3.1%. The higher cost in respect of the former was due to costly procedures associated with administering donor funds.

(*f*) For the PCB, the spread allowed on donor funds at 3 to 4 per cent was inadequate to cover the lending costs on such loans. It had to make up the deficits from its other loaning activities.

Overall, this experience shows that the source of funding has a strong influence on the composition of loan portfolios, lending costs, and quality of lending. When financial intermediaries rely on local deposits, they tend to be more efficient in evaluating loans. Consequently delinquencies in them end to be comparatively less. Public institutions, especially those which depend on external funding, tend to overcentralize their operations, resulting in high administrative costs.

The Caisse Nationale de Crédit Agricole (CNCA) in Morocco (Currency Dirham: DH)

CNCA was established in 1962 as a government-owned agricultural development bank. It is one of the successful organizational innovations to meet the credit needs of small farmers. Some of the special features of CNCA which contributed to its success are as follows:

(*a*) It operates two types of branch offices at the regional level: Caisse Regionale de Crédit Agricole (CRCA), which lends to large farmers, co-operatives, and other groups, and Caisse Locale de Crédit Agricole (CLCA), which lends to small farmers (defined as those who earn between US$23 and $1750 per annum at 1976 prices).

(*b*) Loan approval authority is decentralized and each branch can approve loans up to a certain level without confirmation from headquarters.

(*c*) CLCA appraisal procedures are simple and are based primarily on desk reviews, unlike CRCA procedures.

(*d*) Credit to small farmers is issued in cash, primarily for cereal production and livestock fattening. Interest rate around 13 per cent has been positive in real terms over the years.

(*e*) Each year small farmers declare for tax purposes the amount of land, number of animals, and fruit trees they own. CLCA branch credit committee decides credit eligibility on the basis of these annual tax assessments.

(*f*) CLCA's recovery is nearly 80 per cent. While taking loans, the farmer has to provide the personal guarantee of another farmer in the area or of a government official as co-signer. In addition the borrower pledges his assets to CLCA. When defaults occur without genuine reasons these assets are expropriated by CLCA through administrative rather than legal action.

(g)   A one-time charge of 2 per cent is levied by CLCA on all loans at the time of disbursement to build up a 'losses guarantee fund'. Over time, sufficient funds have been accumulated in the fund to cover all inherent risks.

(h)   The dividend due on state capital is retained by CNCA to strengthen the equity base and generate more funds for further lending.

(i)   CNCA started from 1970 a programme of savings mobilization in the rural areas through mobile units called 'banking counters'.

(j)   Due to CNCA's overall operational efficiency, reduced expenditure on staff, and increased interest income, its net operating income at DH2.9 million during 1978–9 increased to DH51.3 million by 1982–3.

CNCA is a success story of building self-sustaining rural financial institutions. Decentralized operations, sound lending procedures, and positive interest rates have contributed to this. There is also strong government backing for CNCA's efforts to enforce good financial discipline and to achieve high levels of loan recovery. At the same time government has allowed CNCA a large degree of independence and autonomy in making credit and management decisions.

Regional Rural Banks in India (RRBs)
(Currency Rupees: Rs)

In 1975 the Government of India appointed a working group to review the problems of institutional credit to the rural disadvantaged. The group found that the existing rural credit agencies – commercial banks and co-operatives – were deficient in many ways to meet the credit needs of the rural poor. They recommended the setting up of State-sponsored, regionally based, and rural oriented banks called Regional Rural Banks (RRBs). The idea was to combine the advantages of both co-operatives and commercial banks, the local feel of the former and the professional outlook of the latter, in the proposed new system, without inheriting their drawbacks.

Each RRB is identified and sponsored by a public sector commercial bank called the Sponsor Bank (SB) in consultation with the state and central governments. Assistance of SB to RRB takes several forms, such as subscription to share capital, provision of managerial staff, concessional finance, etc. The chairman of an RRB is a senior official of the SB. The share capital of an RRB at Rs2.5 million is subscribed by central government, SB, and state government in the proportion of 50:35:15. A nine-member board of directors, headed by the chairman and comprising three directors each from SB and central government and two from the state government, manages the affairs of each RRB. An RRB operates in one or two districts with homogeneity in agroclimatic conditions and rural clientele. To keep their rural ethos, RRBs draw personnel from local areas and their salary levels are aligned to those of comparable employees in the state government. RRBs are not to emulate the sophisticated look of a commercial bank: they are directed to keep a low-cost profile by economizing on other overheads; however they have the status of scheduled commercial banks and they are eligible to draw refinance from the National Bank. Their deposits carry rates ranging from 9 to 10 per cent and advances 10 to 14 per cent. Most of their lendings are exclusively targeted to the rural poor.

Started as an experimental measure in 1975, the growth of RRBs over the years has been phenomenal. By December 1985 there were 187 RRBs, with 12,000 branches covering 332 districts out of a total of 410 districts in India. Their advances at that date aggregated to Rs13,330 million and deposits to Rs11,590 million. They had around 9 million rural clients as borrowers. The two major problems which have emerged in RRBs are their failure to maintain financial viability and their high overdues. By 1984, 50 RRBs had accumulated losses in excess of their capital. During 1984 only 42 RRBs had made profits, while the remaining 131 had suffered losses. Defaults in RBBs ranged between 40 and 50 per cent of amounts due, similar to co-operatives and commercial banks.

The RRB experiment in India has the following lessons.[7]

(a) If lending is confined exclusively to the rural poor, the institution may not be able to take advantage of scale and scope economies necessary to maintain financial viability.

(b) Low effective margin between borrowing and lending rates would result in erosion of profitability. It would be difficult to make good such losses by external funding on a perpetual basis.

(c) Administrative costs of extending credit to the rural poor is high and it cannot be passed on to anyone else except to the borrowers.

(d) Harping too much on the low-cost profile could be counter-productive. Often lesser costs could mean limited business resulting in low profitability.

(e) It is difficult to develop a well disciplined and committed cadre of field animators. There was a lot of discontent among RRB personnel. They started comparing themselves with SB staff who were often operating the same business round the corner in much better working conditions.

(f) As a concept, combining the good features of co-operatives and commercial banks was sound. But in actual practice, such a hybridization brought in its wake the deficiencies of both systems.

(g) All said and done, RRB is a novel experiment and in a short time it could reach a large number of the rural disadvantaged. However, it proves that even the most innovative experiment in rural credit cannot succeed if it is not self-sustaining.

Annex I

Illustrative allocation of costs and benefits			Scenario I
Costs	*Lender*	*Borrower*	*Society*
A. Transaction costs	6	–	6
B. Transaction costs	–	5	5
C. Cost of capital	3	10	15
D. Defaults	20	–	–
E. Inflation	6	–	6
Total	35	15	32
Benefits			
A. Farm surplus	–	30	40
B. Lending rate	10	–	–
C. Inflation	–	6	–
	10	36	40
Net Benefits	(−25)	+21	+8

			Scenario II
Costs			
A. Transaction costs	3	–	3
B. Transaction costs	–	3	3
C. Cost of capital	9	20	15
D. Defaults	10	–	–
E. Inflation	5	–	–
Total	27	23	21
Benefits			
A. Farm surplus	–	25	35
B. Lending rate	20	–	–
C. Inflation	–	5	–
	20	30	35
Net Benefits	(−7)	+7	+14

Costs			
A. Transaction costs	3	–	3
B. Transaction costs	–	3	3
C. Cost of capital	9	25	15
D. Defaults	5	–	–
E. Inflation	3	–	3
	20	28	24

Benefits			
A. Farm surplus	–	30	30
B. Lending rate	25	–	–
C. Inflation	–	3	–
	25	33	30
Net Benefits	+5	+5	+6

From these illustrations it can be seen that lenders have very limited manoeuvrability. Their only major source of income is the rate of interest charged on loans. The major claims against this are interest payments, lender transaction costs, defaults, and inflation. Even under the most favourable conditions (Scenario III), these costs aggregate to a minimum 20 per cent. In the case of the individual borrower and society as a whole, the rate of return on investment is the crucial factor. This, of course, could vary depending on several factors and fluctuate year by year. On the other hand, lending rates are normally fixed once and for all (with minimum changes) while lender's costs fluctuate widely. In fact even at a much higher lending rate of 25 per cent (Scenario III), it is worth while for the farmer and society to commit resources in view of higher return on investment. At lower rates, it would be unprofitable for the lender to continue lending. It has also to be borne in mind that interest costs generally form only a small proportion of total production costs. For example, a study in Zambia had found that interest costs formed only 10 per cent of production costs.[8] Due to this low weight of interest costs in total costs, it was found that even a doubling of lending rate from 9.5% to 18% would increase overall production costs only by 7%.

Annex II Maximum acceptable loan transaction costs (MALTC)
Assumptions
- (a) Loan size $100,000
- (b) Equity $1000
- (c) External source/deposits $90,000
- (i) Cost of borrowed funds (8% interest) = 7200
- (ii) Loss due to defaults (98% recovery) = 2000
- (iii) Earning from lendings (14% interest) = 14000
- (iv) Net income iii – (i+ii) = 4800
- (v) Maximum acceptable loan transaction costs = 4800/100,000 = 4.8%

Impact of Changes		*(MALTC)*
A. Increase in lending rate to 18%	=	8.6%
B. Increases in defaults by 2%	=	2.8%
C. Increase in cost of borrowed funds to 10%	=	3.0%

Annex III Impact on Financing Institutions

Factor	Viability	Self-sufficiency	Accessibility	Efficiency
1. Larger turnover	+	?	0	0
2. Increase in lending rate	++	?	+	0
3. Increase in resource costs	–	–	0	0
4. Emphasis on savings	+	++	+	0
5. New technology	?	?	++	0
6. Innovative lending experiments	+	0	++	+
7. Improved loan recovery	+	++	0	0
8. Inflation	–	–	?	?
9. Committed bank agents	0	0	++	+
10. Streamlining of lending procedures	?	?	+	++
11. Reduction in transaction costs of lender	+	0	+	+
12. Reduction in transaction costs of borrower	0	0	++	0
13. Decollaterization	0	0	++	0
14. Insurance cover of bank loans	+	?	+	0

Factor	Viability	Self-sufficiency	Accessibility	Efficiency
15. Insurance cover of assets financed	0	0	++	0
16. People's participation	0	0	++	?

+ = positive contribution
++ = substantial positive contribution
– = negative effect
0 = no effect
? = uncertain

CHAPTER 14
Lessons for Rural Bankers and Policy Makers

If to do were as easy as to know what were
good to do, Chapels had been Churches, and
poor men's cottages princes' palaces.

SHAKESPEARE

THE PRINCIPAL agencies who are to initiate action on various issues discussed in the foregoing chapters are donor agencies, governments, central banks, financing agencies, and the borrowers. What are the lessons that they can draw from this analysis? What steps can and need they take to revitalize their rural financial markets and institutions? At the risk of some repetition, a specific action programme for each of them is outlined below. Needless to say that they are closely linked with each other and some action may have to be pursued simultaneously by different agencies. As countries and rural financial markets markedly vary, some of the suggestions may not be relevant in certain situations, some may need modifications, and some others, even when relevant, may not be politically acceptable. Despite these limitations, the action programme is presented here to serve as a guide to rural bankers and policy makers. Ultimately it is their perception and willingness to initiate action that really matters, and not the quality of analysis and writings of committed academics. Of course the latter could influence the former, but by itself it may not be of much use in fine-tuning the rural financial markets. There is one more reason for suggesting a concrete action programme. It has been observed that although problems encountered by different credit programmes across the developing world have great similarities, the 'Winner's Profile' often varied from country to country. This indicated that there was ample scope for learning from one another's mistakes and strengths. What is contained in these sections should not, however, be viewed in isolation from earlier chapters.

Donor agencies

1. The setting up of new rural financial institution's credit projects should not be viewed as a panacea for all rural credit problems. Instead they should place more emphasis on the improvement of financial intermediation process. This would be possible only when they study the rural financial market of a country in its totality instead of isolated rural finance issues and institutions.

2.   They should judge the rural financial market of a country not just by the increase in volume of loans extended but by other indicators, such as rural savings mobilized, range of financial services extended, accessibility to rural population, flexibility of operations, and ability to achieve financial viability.

3.   It is not the volume of donor assistance but the appropriate policy changes it can bring in the recipient countries that is more important. Anyway, since most of the rural credit is extended to purchase local goods (this can be met by increase in money supply), donor loans which support them in effect become balance-of-payments assistance. A proper blend of project loans and sector loans would be more relevant from the point of view of improving the policies of recipients.

4.   Donor agencies can greatly help the rural bankers and policy makers to assess the specific problems of rural financial markets. They can fund training programmes, seminars, etc. for them, to stimulate discussion on issues relating to policy and implementation.

5.   Donor agencies can fund the following activities:

(a)   Start-up cost of financing institutions wanting to broaden their financial services.
(b)   Experiments to test financial innovations.
(c)   Additional research capacity in central banks and financial institutions.
(d)   Exchange of visits of rural credit experts from one country to another.
(e)   Computers and other similar equipment which can be used for developing new management information systems.
(f)   Training costs of loan agents and other middle level officials.
(g)   Research to promote new rural technologies.

6.   Donor agencies can provide help in the development of training institutions for middle and lower level rural bankers. Development of curriculums, teaching material, audio-visual aids, training of trainers, etc. can be done with the assistance of experts from donor agencies.

7.   Donor agencies can help standardize various terminologies and ratios currently being used in rural banking, so that information on individual countries would be more directly comparable. Some of the concepts which need standardization are loan arrear ratios, average borrowing rates, average lending rates, margin, profitability index, break-even point, turnover, lender and borrower transaction costs, etc. Donor agencies can also fix broadly acceptable ranges of costs relating to administration, and staff.

110

8. Donor agencies could initiate the setting up of an International Institute of Rural Financial Institutions (IIRFI) to facilitate international exchange of ideas and experiences. Donor agencies, the World Bank, regional development banks, FAO, regional agricultural credit associations, governments and Apex rural credit institutions in the developing countries could become members of that institution. An IIRFI essentially should be a research and training institution (and not a financing body), like the Institute of Development Studies (University of Sussex) in England, where rural bankers and policy makers could meet to exchange ideas and experiences.

National governments

1. Governments should use rural financial markets for more efficient allocation of scarce national resources. When the overall structure of the economy is conducive to greater inequality, they should not attempt to bring equality in income and assets just through rural credit policies, without correcting other macro-economic policies causing such distortions.

2. A policy to push rural credit should be supported by a policy to make the activities supported by credit sufficiently remunerative. In other words, the overall pricing policy relating to inputs and outputs should be such that rural activities are remunerative enough for the borrowers.

3. Promotion of viable technologies through research is important. Such technologies should be well tested and appropriate to the field conditions. Credit can play its legitimate role only when there are opportunities generated in the economy through technology.

4. Supporting services like input supply, extension, marketing, and training should be linked to these new activities through a well-thought-out plan.

5. There is no one ideal blueprint of rural credit structure applicable under all circumstances. It is often easier and more productive to orient an existing institution than to create a new one. New institutions need be created only when it is absolutely essential. Any experiment in the field of rural credit should be allowed to run for a period of time. Frequent changes in policy and institutional structure will only undermine the confidence of rural people, particularly the small farmers, in formal institutions.

6. Subsidies to new institutions and projects may be necessary to make them self-sustaining. But any such support should be temporary

111

and conditional. In any case, it should not lead to a sense of complacency and tendency to expect perpetual support from government. The best way would be to work out a predetermined plan for progressive reduction of subsidies.

7. Government intervention in financial institutions should be minimal and indirect. A sense of autonomy combined with accountability is the best way to ensure good performance. This also implies that governments should not impose indiscriminate loan targets on financial institutions.

8. Creation of self-sustaining rural financial institutions should be the primary aim of governments' rural credit policies. This would be possible only if the lending rates are sufficiently high to defray lending costs. Any real lending rate below 18 per cent is not likely to meet this objective under most circumstances. Hence govenments should attempt progressively to revise lending rates to reach this level.

9. Instead of mandating to lend to the rural poor, governments should create an environment under which such lending becomes a business proposition and attractive to financial agencies. Under such conditions both private banks and government banks would take to rural lending willingly. Wholesale remission of debts, insistence on very low interest rates, policy statements discouraging farmers from repaying loans, etc. can vitiate this environment.

10. Governments can help the financial institutions by taking the following steps.

(*a*) Provision of appropriate legislative support for rural lending.
(*b*) Encouraging NGOs to intermediate between financial institutions and rural clients.
(*c*) Ensuring legal guarantee of ownership of properties, through land survey, registration, etc.
(*d*) Provision of selective guarantees such as price and purchase guarantees, crop and livestock insurance, guarantees indemnifying institutions against loan defaults, etc.

Central banks

1. Central banks can monitor closely the rural financial systems only by setting up specialized rural finance departments. They should encourage a range of institutions (competing with each other) to operate in the rural financial markets.

2. Monetary and credit policies should be conducive to the promotion of efficient rural financial systems. Such policies should promote investment in agriculture, reduce defaults, and mobilize rural savings.

3. Central banks have a major role in fixing interest rates. While stipulating nominal rates for the rural sector they should take into account: (a) normal return on investments; (b) rate of inflation; (c) interest in the informal system; (d) spread necessary between rates on savings and lendings; and (f) premium necessary on longer term loans vis-à-vis short-term loans.

4. Central banks should liaise effectively between governments and the rural financial institutions. For this purpose, central banks should collect and disseminate information relating to important aspects of the working of rural financial markets, relevant to policy decisions. These relate to:

(a) The extent of voluntary financial savings mobilized by the rural financial institutions, cost of such mobilization, related problems and issues.

(b) Loan repayment performance under different credit programmes, related problems and issues.

(c) Costs and benefits of various financial innovations and services.

(d) Term structure, loan size, and beneficiaries of rural loans.

(e) Variations in nominal and real rate of interest over a period of time.

(f) Variations in formal agricultural credit stocks and flows including changes over time in the ratio of agricultural credit to total credit and agricultural credit to the agricultural output.

(g) Inter-regional and inter-sectoral flows of financial claims. Central banks should promote effective discussion of these issues among government officials, rural bankers, etc. through seminars and workshops.

5. Central banks should set up an effective supervisory and inspection service for the rural financial systems. Such checks and balances, if properly instituted, can inspire the confidence of the rural community, particularly that of the rural depositors in the formal financial systems.

6. Central banks should extend rediscount facilities to rural financial institutions in such a way that they promote self-sufficiency in resources in the latter over a period of time. In any case, access to rediscount should not dampen their efforts to mobilize rural savings.

7. When funds from donor agencies are channelled through central banks, it should be ensured that ultimate lending institutions get sufficient operative margin to administer the loans.

8. Central banks can arrange to set up deposit insurance schemes to protect people's savings and credit guarantee schemes to protect financial institutions against defaults.

9.   Central banks can help the financial institutions in setting up systems for following activities: (a) manpower resource management; (b) training of senior, middle, and lower level managers; (c) monitoring and evaluation of rural credit programmes; (d) accounting and financial management; (e) management information; (f) data gathering and anaylsis based on standard definitions and criteria.

10.   Central banks can devise methods that help rural financial institutions to manage their risk and liquidity problems better. Stipulations regarding debt–equity ratios and statutory reserves, and facilities such as inter-bank lending arrangements and rediscounting can be appropriately structured to meet this objective.

11.   Central banks can promote research on important rural financial issues relating to (a) optimum level of administrative costs; (b) standardization of financial ratios; (c) inflation projections for interest rate analysis; (d) consumer preference regarding financial instruments; (e) range of potential financial services necessary for specific rural markets; (f) design and evaluation of savings campaigns; (g) methods of linking formal and informal agencies; (h) innovative methods to take banking to rural areas and the rural poor. Central banks should also help financing agencies to develop their own research capacity on some of these issues.

12.   When a number of rural financing agencies operate in a country it will be the duty of the central bank to co-ordinate their operations. Such co-ordination can be achieved through presenting guidelines for branch expansion, for preparation of area credit plans, etc. Creation of a body like the Technical Board for Agricultural Credit in the Philippines can help in such co-ordination.

Financing institutions

1.   Achievement of financial viability and self-sufficiency in resources should be the principal objective of any financial institution. They should at the same time increase accessibility to rural clients and build their confidence in the formal financial system. Rural savings mobilization, efficient loan administration, better resource management, reduction in defaults, innovative lending experiments, improving range of services, etc. should be viewed in this broad context. Institutional objectives based on these principles should be made clear to all those who work in them.

2.   The rural sector and in particular the rural disadvantaged should be viewed as a market to be developed through appropriate financial technologies rather than as a welfare proportion to satisfy government mandates.

114

3. Financial institutions should reduce their transaction costs on deposit mobilization and loan administration through innovative experiments. Group lending, mobile credit officers, one-man rural branches, etc. are some of the measures to reduce costs without reducing accessibility to small farmers. Such costs can also be reduced through streamlining administrative procedures, devising appropriate management information systems, mechanization, decentralization of operations, etc.

4. The efficiency of financial institutions should be improved through better manpower planning. A sound system of manpower resource management should embrace recruitment, training, placement, job specification and evaluation, accountability, incentives, and punishments. Just as policies cannot march ahead of institutions, institutions cannot march ahead of their personnel. Setting rigorous standards relating to staff rewards and accountability can substantially improve the performance of financial institutions.

5. Financial institutions can improve their accessibility to rural clients by creating a motivated cadre of field animators, who act as a link between financial institutions and rural clientele. Field animators should be trained to act as guide, philosopher, and friend in managing their resources. Thus instead of the conventional 'supervised credit' they should be able to provide a new form of 'counselled credit' to rural borrowers.

6. Similarly, simplified loan formalities, speedy loan evaluation and loan decision, decollaterization, spread of rural outlets, etc. can decrease borrower transaction costs and consequently increase confidence in the formal system. Often disbursement in kind could also be of much help to borrowers, particularly when they are illiterate and unfamiliar with cash transactions.

7. Just as small loans raise average operational costs, an increase in the number of loans can bring it down. Hence, financial institutions should try to cover all types of clients in the farm and non-farm sector in their operational area. To avoid pre-emption of loans by big borrowers in such cases, specific measures may be devised. Identification of activities for the rural poor, earmarking a specific share of credit for them, prescribing a separate application form, simplifying appraisal procedures relating to small loans, etc. can be tried. Identification of the rural disadvantaged should be based on criteria such as income, asset holding, location, and activity. Such criteria should be clear and unambiguous so that they can be put into operation by field agents.

8. Financial institutions should try to broaden their range of assets and liabilities. This can be done by covering different types of clients, in

115

the farm and non-farm sectors, by mixing short, medium, and long-term loans, and by borrowing from different sources. Such a combination will help them to manage their resources more efficiently.

9. The operating margin available to financial institutions should be able to cover their transaction costs. In other words, lending rates should be fixed in such a way as to cover (a) interest paid on borrowings including deposits; (b) administrative costs; (c) decapitalization through inflation; (d) defaults; and (e) a reasonable margin of profits to build reserves. Real lending rates below 18 per cent are unlikely to cover these costs under most circumstances.

10. Financial institutions should place added emphasis on the mobilization of voluntary rural savings. The performance of lenders that accept deposits would be significantly better than those who do not. The former will be able to reduce transaction costs and also loan delinquency as compared with the latter. Offering attractive interest rates, providing convenient savings instruments, improving range of financial services, devising innovative methods of savings promotion, instituting staff incentive schemes, etc. are some of the ways through which rural savings can be mobilized.

11. Delinquencies and defaults should be handled tactfully. Flexibility in genuine cases and strict enforcement of sanctions in the case of wilful defaults can be a good policy. Incentives for prompt repayment by borrowers and penalty for delays could work well. Incentives to loan agents for better recovery performance can also be tried. It is essential to devise a proper accounting system which would show how much is due from whom and for how long. To meet loan rescheduling demands arising out of natural calamities etc. special funds may be set up.

12. Information relating to loans, deposits, turnover, interest rates, margins, transactions costs, repayment, etc. should be promptly available for comparison and policy decisions. Overall the emphasis of the management information system should be on the quality of the information rather than on the quantity. Use of computers and other mechanized systems can speed up information and consequently improve quality of decisions.

13. For a rural borrower, family and farm are not mutually exclusive entities. Deficit in one affects the other. Hence credit should be given within his overall debt capacity to meet all his needs including genuine consumption needs. Promise of such 'total credit' will improve his confidence in the formal system and also facilitate better recoveries.

14. Simple and effective ways for disseminating information on credit and savings schemes among illiterate rural clients should be developed. Using local images and expressions can be very effective in this respect.

15.   Financial institutions should place added emphasis on imparting training to potential borrowers so that the latter will be familiar with their rights and responsibilities regarding bank credit. Such training, apart from improving their ability to manage their assets and funds, will also promote better people's participation in credit programmes.

16.   Formal agencies should try to learn from the ways of the informal money lender and adopt them to the extent they are practicable in an institutional system. In selected cases the informal system could be used to provide agencies of the formal institutions.

Borrowers

1.   The success of some of the traditional savings and credit associations points to the fact that for building effective rural credit systems at grassroots level, the initiative must come from the rural people themselves. Therefore it would be necessary to create an environment and incentives for such initiatives, partly by people themselves and partly through state intervention.

2.   Field agents and local leaders can effectively promote such local initiatives and participation. In such cases, care should be taken to see that new dependent relationships are not substituted for old ones. No individual leader, however charismatic, should be allowed to manage a programme without developing a second tier of leaders.

3.   Borrowers should be able to view rural credit agencies as partners in their own development instead of as a benevolent and paternalistic external intervention to be exploited.

4.   Rural borrowers should participate in the activities of the financing agency. The system of co-operatives affords maximum scope for such participation. People can participate by becoming members of the management committees, by forming associations of depositors and borrowers, etc. There should be constant dialogue between the lenders and borrowers regarding problems confronted.

5.   Borrower education and training is one way to promote people's participation. Borrowers should be educated in the following areas: (a) formalities associated with institutional loans; (b) effective management of finance; (c) maintenance of assets created out of credit; (d) rights and responsibilities associated with bank credit; (e) entrepreneurship development.

6.   Borrowers should respect the covenants of credit institutions, particularly those relating to repayment.

CHAPTER 15
Conclusions

Time is the king of men. He is both their parent,
and he is their grave: And gives them what he
will, and not what they crave!

SHAKESPEARE

FINANCIAL behaviour is a part of economic behaviour which otherwise consists of choosing and managing alternatives in production, consumption, and marketing. Thus financial management closely interacts with other economic behaviour. Limited net worth, irregular flow of incomes, lack of opportunities, etc. affect the choices of the small producer relating to production, consumption, and marketing. These special characteristics affect the nature and scope of his financial behaviour and his influence on the organizations dealing with them. Consequently delivering credit effectively to rural people becomes a complex process often not appreciated or understood. In a way, of all the services, rural credit is the most difficult to deliver. The problem is compounded by the fungibility of money, which makes directing it to a pre-determined activity, person, or area less effective without an appropriate policy environment. Such a policy for institutional credit is mostly the outcome of the political, economic, and social system of the country, in which financial institutions are deeply embedded. Often they cannot by themselves undo the damaging impacts of macro-level policies pursued, and if these constraints are severe, it will be difficult for any financial institution to operate successfully.

It is against this background that one should view the two distinct strategies relating to rural credit which have emerged over the years; the one supported by USAID and some other donors like the World Bank and the other pursued by IFAD and certain other agencies. The former focuses on the creation of a proper development environment by emphasizing market prices, economic incentives, and viability of institutions. Such a macro-treatment is thought necessary to cure the development constraints relating to technology, research, extension, and other supporting services. This emphasis on national economic policies assumes that once *'prices'* are right, *'investment opportunities'* are created, and *'viable institutions'* fostered small farmers would benefit automatically. The second strategy concentrates on projects that *'organize the poor'* at the grassroots level through field animators and then provide them directly with the necessary *'resources'* – capital, technology, and other supporting services. This approach stems from the

118

belief that overall price, financial market, and institutional reforms would benefit all farmers, largely the big farmers to the neglect of small farmers. It reasons that if the poor lack access to resources, there is no way by which they can benefit from such macro-level policy interventions. Thus they see USAID's approach as too macro-oriented to benefit the rural poor.

An attempt is made here to show that these two points of view are not necessarily irreconcilable. It is possible to achieve a 'golden mean' between these two conflicting positions. While USAID's aims may be highly desirable, it is questionable whether they are attainable in the short term in many developing countries. On the other hand, the major problems with the IFAD approach are the financial viability of lending agencies and universal replicability of certain grassroots-level organizations. It will be difficult to support such efforts through external aid perpetually. At the same time, it has to be reckoned that without proper economic policies the resources which have reached the poor at high costs may not be productive enough. An approach which does not sacrifice the attainable for the ideal and attacks both macro- and micro-level constraints seems much more practical and relevant. How this optimum mix between the two approaches is to be arrived at, would depend on individual country circumstances. It would be necessary to build on the strengths of local institutions. A committed cadre of field animators should be developed to dispense what may be termed 'counselled credit' as against the conventional 'supervised credit'. This shift from 'partial credit' to 'total credit' should be reinforced by policies that foster self-sustaining financial institutions. Improving the range of services, increasing the loan turnover, reducing transaction costs, mobilizing rural savings, containing loan defaults, revising interest rates, etc. should form part of this package. Demand for productive credit can be generated only when new opportunities spring up through application of new technologies. Policy constraints which made these activities less remunerative should be removed over a period of time.

The success of any rural credit programme depends on the consistency and co-ordination of decisions taken by three parties: the borrowing farmer, the lending institution, and the national government. When these parties have different and conflicting objectives, achieving this consistency becomes difficult. For example: when costs are hidden and diffused and benefits readily visible, rural credit institutions become vulnerable to political intrusion. As one comprehensive rural credit survey in India noted, 'We have in the course of our enquiry found rural credit to be an extraordinary complex of needs, purposes, fulfilments, and frustrations. It is surrounded and interpenetrated by many forces. These are economic, sociological, institutional, and so on; and while some of these are obvious, many of them are usually almost unsuspected.'

In fact experience shows that impressionistic and intuitive conclusions in the field of rural credit are often erroneous. A plenitude of asserted truths could, on closer examination, dissolve into no more than a myth and illusion. Considering the large number of rural credit programmes (disbursing approximately US $ 40 billion annually) which have been mounted around the developing world to meet the credit needs of farmers, it is surprising that reliable data to guide policy are relatively scanty. This poor information base may be due to the extremely complex web of relationships among institutions involved directly with lending and indirectly with providing supporting services on the one hand, and among the various economic sectors, political interests, and social structures on the other. It is here that the role of rural financial experts assumes importance to clear the air and bring out the issues as objectively as possible, not being swayed by the philosophical intentions of policy makers. As in any field of enquiry, experience is a good guide in the field of rural credit also: interacting with different experiences is possible only when one is aware of them. This attempt to put together some of the experiences is based on that conviction. But as situations, constraints, strengths, and weaknesses differ considerably from region to region, one cannot look for a blueprint that would work in all regions. The presence of such diversity points to the need for improvisation and acclimatization based on a cross-country flow of information, ideas, and experiences. For better or worse, rural credit will continue to be a powerful mechanism in most developing countries to stimulate development, particularly that of the rural disadvantaged. Through a spirit of enquiry and experimentation, preparedness for adjustment and adaptation, rural financial experts should see that it goes for the better.

Notes

Chapter 1: The Process of Financial Intermediation

1 For a brief discussion of the role of financial innovations in economic development, see Bhatt, 1979, pp. 95–126.
2 For a discussion of rural financial intermediation, see Adams, 'Effects of Finance on Rural Development', in Adams *et al.*, 1984, pp. 11–21.

Chapter 2: The Role of Credit in Rural Development

1 See Penny, 1968, pp. 32–45.
2 For a discussion of the nature of capital, see Fisher, *Capital and Income*, ch. 4.
3 Lavington, 1934. For a detailed discussion of the relationship between capital and credit, see Belshaw, 1931, pp. 3–15.
4 Galbraith, 1952, p. 31.
5 Patrick, 1966, pp. 174–89.
6 Fungibility as defined as 'of such a kind or nature that one specimen or part may be used in place of another specimen or equal part . . . interchangeable'.

Chapter 3: The Evolution of Rural Credit Policies

1 Walinsky, 1963, p. 145.
2 Bathrick, 1981, pp. 5–7.
3 World Bank, 1975.
4 FAO, *Report on the World Conference on Credit for Farmers in Developing Countries*, 1975.
5 Miller, 1975.
6 US Agency for International Development, 1973.
7 *Ibid.*, 1985, Appendix A.
8 *Ibid.*, 1973, vol. 18, no. SR 118, Evaluation Paper 6, p. 25.
9 World Bank, *op. cit.*, p. 17.

Chapter 4: Why Credit for the Rural Disadvantaged?

1 See Bauer and Yamey, 1957, ch. 14, 'Specific Policy Measures Affecting Agriculture', pp. 209–34.
2 See Lipton, M., 'Rural Credit, Farm Finance and Village Households', in Howell (ed.), 1980 pp. 235–58. He argues that, due to the 'Sen effect', redistribution of loans towards smaller family enterprises would increase their contribution to total output and that rate of return to extra credit would be greater on smaller farms.
3 Wortman, 1976, pp. 35–6.
4 McNamara, 1973.

5 US Agency for International Development, 1973, vol. 19, no. SR 119. See the portion relating to working definition 'Small Farmers'.
6 Donald, 1976, section relating to 'What is a Small Farmer?', pp. 15–17.
7 International Fund for Agricultural Development, 1985, p. 37.
8 Von Pischke *et al.* (eds.), 1983, p. 366.
9 This was also confirmed by the All India Debt and Investment Survey (1971–2). About 63 per cent of total outstanding debt was accounted for by 30 per cent of the rural households with assets of Rs 10,000 and above. Overall, non-institutional sources had provided about 70 per cent of rural household loans in 1971. Almost the entire debt of agricultural labourers (96 per cent) and artisans (95 per cent) was accounted for by non-institutional lenders.

Chapter 5: The Current Debate on Rural Financial Markets

1 Patrick, 1966, pp. 174–89.
2 Penny, 1968, pp. 32–45. In his view, the credit will be effective only when the peasants have the ability and willingness to put the additional funds to productive uses.
3 Adams, 1971.
4 For a brief review of historical views on rural financial markets, criticism of the current assumptions, and suggestions for policy changes, see Adams, 1979.
5 For an overview of agricultural credit policy in developing countries, see Schaefer-Kehnert and von Pischke, 1986. The bibliography at the end provides useful references.
6 Adams, 'Small Farmer Credit Programmes', 1978.
7 *Ibid.*, 'Rural Financial Markets: The Case Against Cheap Credit', 1986. The paper gives a brief summary of the new strategy. Also Adams in Asian Productivity Organisation, 1984.
8 Samaranayake, 1986, pp. 22–31. On the basis of Sri Lankan experience he argues that interest rate policy is not an effective monetary instrument for allocating resources to productive users.
9 Lipton, 1976, pp. 543–53.

Chapter 6: The Structure of Financial Institutions

1 Von Pischke, 1980, pp. 79–81. He discusses the performance problems of such specialized banks set up to finance agriculture.
2 Robert, 1979, pp. 163–84. He argues that the growth of the co-operative in India was the result of economic and political benefits derived by the village elite, Indian politicians, and the British government.
3 See also Youngjohns, B. J., 'Co-operatives and Credit: a Re-examination', in Howell (ed.), 1980, pp. 179–98. According to him, Indian co-operatives were viewed not so much as worth while in themselves or to their members, but as instruments for public policy. This 'instrumental' approach to co-operatives, which spread throughout the world, was the root cause of the failure of co-operatives.
4 Reserve Bank of India, 1969, ch. 33, p. 971. Also Reserve Bank of India, 1985.
5 Meyer, 1985, Annex III, p. 21.

Chapter 7: Mobilization of Resources

1 Rahman, 1986, pp. 18–23.
2 Meyer, 1985, Annex III. See also Vogel and Burkett, 1986. According to

them: 'Transaction costs, as well as yields and liquidity, appear to be crucial determinants of the demand for financial assets, especially among low income savers. This is because of the essential role of working capital management in determining the asset portfolios and income levels of these households. If transaction costs of deposits are high, then small savers will be deterred from using them and rely on either cash or real goods for working capital. Thus, successful small saver programs will have to make deposits easily accessible, cut down on paper work and lines etc.'

3 Fry, 1984.
4 Elegalas, 1978, pp. 437–50.
5 Mittendorf, 1985, pp. 275–91.
6 Grima, 1978
7 Bouman, 1977, pp. 181–214.
8 Ong et al., 1976, pp. 578–81.
9 Adams, 1984. He argues that mobilization of voluntary financial savings has five advantages. It improves resource allocation, helps in more equitable income distribution, leads to financial market viability, dampens inflation, and expands economic freedom.

Chapter 8: Issues in Loan Administration

1 For a discussion of various types of credit, see Miller, 1975, pp. 6–14.
2 See Mollett, 1984.
3 The concept of debt capacity is dealt with in detail in von Pischke, 'Improving Donor Intervention in Rural Finance', in Adams et al. (eds), 1984, pp. 287–90.
4 See International Fund for Agricultural Development, 1985.
5 Chambers, 1974.
6 A research study done among 250 farm households in six villages of Sambalpur District in Orissa (India) during 1981–2, found the borrower transaction cost as high as 10 per cent for smaller loans as shown below:

Land holding in acres	Average loan size Rs	Percentage of Borrower Transaction Cost
up to 1.25	581	9.76
1.26 – 2.50	1240	4.00
2.51–500	1629	3.13
5.01 – 10.00	3666	1.05
10.01 – above	8075	0.56

7 See Donald, 1976, pp. 118–19. It was found that bankers in north-east Brazil, a low income farming area, incurred losses on loans less than US$2000, while in Taiwan farmers' associations made profits on loans one quarter of that value. The key difference was loan volume: several hundreds in the case of the former and several thousand in the case of the latter. Thus the most important way to reduce average cost was to increase the number of customers through improving small farmers' access to credit programmes.
8 For a practical guide in setting up monitoring and evaluation systems in lending institutions, see International Fund for Agricultural Development, 1984.

Chapter 9: Reaching the Rural Disadvantaged

1 Lipton, 1979, p. 351.
2 See Chambers, 1983, pp. 92–101. He argues that to combine the knowledge of

the professional outsider and the conventional wisdom of the rural people, it would be necessary for outsiders to step down off their pedestals and sit down, listen, and learn.

3 For a discussion of some of the issues on group lending, see International Labour Office, 1984.

4 See Carroll, Thomas F., 'Group Credit for Small Farmers', US Agency for International Development, 1973, vol. 19, no. SR 119, pp. 265–82.

5 See Adams, 'The Economics of Loans to Informal Groups', 1978; see also Adams and Ladman, 1979, pp. 85–92.

6 See Oxby, 1981.

7 See Eggar, 1986, pp. 447–62.

8 For a detailed analysis of the INVIERNO project, see Bathrick, 1981, pp. 39–130.

9 Reserve Bank of India, 1981, pp. 59–63.

Chapter 10: Delinquencies and Default Problems

1 US Agency for International Development, 1985, p. 46.

2 For a discussion of the main elements of costs associated with defaults in the Indian co-operatives, see Datey, 1978, pp. 13–16.

3 Sanderatne, 1978, pp. 290–304.

4 Adyemo, 1984, p. 270.

6 World Bank, 1975, pp. 40–2.

6 See Reserve Bank of India, 1974, p. 224.

7 See Padmanabhan, *CERES*, 1986, pp. 26–31.

8 See Kwadwo, 1979.

9 Donald, 1976, pp. 137–58.

10 See Stickley, T., and E. Tapsoba, 'Loan Repayment Delinquency in Upper Volta', in Howell (ed.), 1989, pp. 273–85.

11 See Vogel, 1981, pp. 58–65.

12 See Sacay *et al.*, 1985, pp. 35–44.

Chapter 11: The Profitable Deployment of Credit

1 US Agency for International Development, 1985, p. 23.

2 See Zambia, Republic of, 1983, pp. 70–3.

3 Lipton, 1977, p. 299.

4 See International Fund for Agricultural Development, 1985, pp. 59–60.

5 Levitsky and Prasad, 1987.

6 Reserve Bank of India, 1954, p. 330.

7 see Sacay *et al.*, 1985, pp. 17–33.

8 See Reserve Bank of India, 1981, pp. 181–97. This review suggested a number of improvements to make DCPs effective.

Chapter 12: Informal Financial Systems

1 See Reserve Bank of India, 1954, pp. 171–2.

2 See Donald, 1976, pp. 84–5.

3 See Nisbet, 1967, pp. 73–90.

4 See Padmanabhan, Pune, 1986, pp. 126–35.

5 See Proceedings of the Seminar conducted by the Asian Productivity Organisation, 1984, p. 202.

6 Harris, 'Money and Commodities, Monopoly and Competition', in Howell (ed.), 1980, pp. 107–29.

7 See Wells, 1980.

8 Lipton, 1979.

9 See Barton, C. G., Informal Financial Markets and the Design of Rural Credit Programs', in Bangladesh Bank, 1979, pp. 59–65.

10 BPM had two basic lending rates: 12% per season for unsecured loans and 9% per season for secured loans. (A season is roughly 195 days.) Of this, 4% was paid to the LCC to meet its lending costs. In August 1972, these rates were reduced to 9% and 6% respectively and LCC commission to 3%. Because of the administrative and legal problems experienced in creating a charge on land, most of the loans were in effect unsecured loans. Consequently BPM abolished the distinctions between secured and unsecured loans in September 1973. Simultaneously, interest rates were also reduced to 8.5% (4.25% per season), retaining LCC commission at 3%.

11 See Ladman, J. R., 'Loan Transaction Costs, Credit Rationing and Market Structure, The Case of Bolivia', in Adams *et al.* (eds.), 1984, pp. 104–19.

Chapter 13: Creating Self-Sustaining Rural Financial Institutions

1 For a discussion of the problems of fixing lending rates, see World Bank, 1975, pp. 45–51, and Md Omar Choudhury, 'Critical Rates of Interest for Institutional Lending to Agricultural Sector in Bangladesh', Bangladesh Bank, 1979 PP. 81–99. This paper argues that lending rates for sectors other than agriculture, the agricultural sector in general, and small farmers should be fixed at 22.5%, 25%, and 27.5% respectively. See also Virmani, 1982; one of the conclusions of this paper is that as credit markets differ fundamentally from markets for goods, analysing loan markets according to the theory applicable to the goods market can be misleading.

2 See Meyer, 1985.

3 See Padmanabhan, Pune, 1986, pp. 38–51.

4 For a discussion of the creation of viable rural banking institutions, see Mittendorf, 1986; see also von Pischke and Rouse, 1983, pp. 21–44.

5 Donald, 1976, p. 67.

6 See Cuevas, C. L., and D. H. Graham, 'Agricultural Lending Costs in Honduras', in Adams *et al.* (eds.), 1984, pp. 96–103.

7 See Padmanabhan, 1987, pp. 33–8.

8 See Zambia, Republic of, 1983, pp. 46–7.

Bibliography

Abbott, Graham J., 'National Saving and Financial Development in Asian Developing Countries', *Asian Development Review* 2:2, 1984, pp. 1–22.

Adams, D. W., 'Agricultural Credit in Latin America. A Critical Review of External Funding Policy', *American Journal of Agricultural Economics*, 53, 2, 1971, pp. 163–172.

Adams, D. W. 'Policy Issues in Rural Finance Development', Paper No. 1, Conference on Rural Finance Research, San Diego, California, 1977.

Adams, D. W., 'The Economics of Loans to Informal Groups of Small Farmers in Low Income Countries', *Occasional Paper No. 525*, Agricultural Finance Program, Ohio State University, Oct. 1978.

Adams, D. W., 'Mobilising Household Savings through Rural Financial Markets', *Economic Development and Cultural Change*, 26, 3, 1978, pp. 547–60.

Adams, D. W., 'Small Farmer Credit Programmes and Interest Rate Policies in Low Income Countries', *Economic and Sociology Occasional Paper 496*, Ohio State University, Studies in Rural Finance, April 1978.

Adams, D. W., 'Recent Performance of Rural Financial Markets in Low Income Countries', Ohio State University, Agricultural Finance Program, *Economics and Sociology Occasional Paper 596*, 1979.

Adams, D. W., 'Do Rural Financial Savings Matter?', *Economics and Sociology Occasional Paper No. 1083*, Ohio State University, May 1984.

Adams, D. W., 'The Conundrum of Successful Credit Projects in Floundering Rural Financial Markets', Dept. of AERS. Ohio State University, 18 Oct. 1985.

Adams, D. W., 'Rural Financial Markets: The Case against Cheap Credit', *CERES* FAO Review, no. 109, 19, 1, Jan.–Feb. 1986.

Adams, D. W., Douglas H. Graham, and J. D. von Pischke, *Undermining Rural Development with Cheap Credit*, Westview Press, Boulder, Colorado, 1984.

Adams, D. W., and J. R. Ladman, 'Lending to Rural Poor through Informal Groups: A Promising Financial Market Innovation?', *Savings and Development*, 3, 2, 1979, pp. 85–94.

126

Adams, D. W., and G. I. Nehman, 'Borrowing Costs for Agricultural Loans in Low-income Countries', *Journal of Development Studies*, 15, 2, pp. 165–176.

Adams, D. W., and A. A. Pablo Romero, 'Group Lending to the Rural Poor in the Dominican Republic: A Stunted Innovation', *Canadian Journal of Agricultural Economics*, 29, 2, July 1981.

Adams, D. W., and R. C. Vogel, 'Rural Financial Markets in Low Income Countries: Recent Controversies and Lessons', *World Development*, 14, 4, 1986, pp. 477–87.

Adyemo, Remi, 'Loan Delinquency in Multi-Purpose Co-operative Union in Kwara State, Nigeria', *Savings and Development*, 8, 3, 1984.

Alexander, M. C., and P. J. Scott, 'The Implications of Group Credit for Rural Development in Malawi', paper prepared for East African Agricultural Economics Conference, Lusaka, Zambia, 1974.

Anderson, Robert, 'Rotating Credit Associations in India', *Economic Development and Cultural Change*, 14 (3 April), 1966.

Asian Productivity Organisation, *Farm Credit Situation in Asia*, Tokyo, 1984.

Asian Productivity Organisation, 'Farm Credit in Selected Asian Countries', Report of a Study Mission Conducted in Japan, 30 Aug.–8 Sept. 1984, APO 1985.

Baker, C. B., and V. K. Bhargava, 'Financing Small Farm Development in India', *Australian Journal of Agricultural Economics*, 18, 2, 1974, pp. 102–118.

Bangladesh Bank, 'Problems and Issues of Agricultural Credit and Rural Finance', Deliberations of the International Workshop on providing Financial Services to the Rural Poor, Dacca, Oct. 1978, Bangladesh Bank, Sept. 1979.

Bathrick, David D., *Agricultural Credit for Small Farm Development: Policies and Practices*, Westview Press, Boulder, Colorado, 1981.

Bauer, P. T., and B. S. Yamey, *The Economics of Under-Developed Countries*, Cambridge Economic Handbooks, Cambridge University Press, 1957.

Belshaw, H. *The Provision of Credit with Special Reference to Agriculture*, Auckland University College Texts, no. 1, Cambridge, 1931.

Belshaw, H., 'Agricultural Credit in Economically Underdeveloped Countries', *FAO Agricultural Studies No. 46*, FAO, Rome, 1959.

Benston, G., and C. W. Smith, 'A Transaction Cost Approach to the Theory of Financial Intermediation', *Journal of Finance*, 31 (Spring), 1979.

Bhatt, V. V., *Structure of Financial Institutions*, Vora & Co., Bombay, 1962.

Bhatt, V. V., and Alan R. Row, 'Capital Market Imperfections and Economic Development', *World Bank Staff Working Paper no. 338*, Washington, 1979.

127

Bhatt, V. V., 'Interest Rate: Transaction Costs and Financial Innovations', *Savings and Development*, 3, 2, 1979.

Bottomley, A., 'Interest Rate Determination in Underdeveloped Rural Areas', *American Journal of Economics*, 57, 2, 1975. pp. 279–91.

Bouman, F. J. A., 'Indigenous Savings and Credit Societies in the Third World: A Message', *Savings and Development*, 1, 4, 1977, pp. 181–214.

Bouman, F. J. A., 'The Rosca: Financial Technology of an Informal Savings and Credit Institution in Developing Economies', *Savings and Development*, 3, 4, 1979, pp. 253–76.

Chambers, Robert, *Managing Rural Development: Ideas and Experiences from East Africa*, Scandinavian Institute of African Studies, Uppsala, 1974.

Chambers, Robert, *Rural Development: Putting the Last First*, Longman, 1983.

Chandavarkar, A. G., 'Interest Rate Policies in Developing Countries', *Finance and Development*, 7, 1, 1970, pp. 19–27.

Chandavarkar, A. G., 'The Non-Institutional Financial Sector in Developing Countries: Macroeconomic Implications for Savings Policies', *Savings and Development* No. 2, 1985.

Chandavarkar, A. G., 'Impact of Monetization and Commercialization of the Subsistence Sector on Savings and Credit in Rural Areas', Report of the International Symposium on the Mobilization of Personal Savings in Developing Countries, Jamaica, United Nations, New York, 1981.

Chandavarkar, A. G., 'Some Aspects of Interest Rate Policies in Less Developed Economies', *IMF Staff Paper 18*, (1 March) 1971.

Datey, C. D. 'The Financial Cost of Agricultural Credit: A Case Study of Indian Experience', *World Bank Staff Working Paper, No. 296*, World Bank, Oct. 1978.

Deutsche Gesellschaft für Technische Zusammenarbeit (GTZ) GmbH, *Cameroon Rural Finance Sector Study*, July 1986.

Donald, Gordon, *Credit for Small Farmers in Developing Countries* Westview Press, Boulder, Colorado, 1976.

Eggar, Philippe, 'Banking for the Rural Poor: Lessons from Some Innovative Savings and Credit Schemes', *ILO Review*, 125, 4, July–Aug. 1986.

Elegalas, P. O., 'The Queueing Cost of Banking in Lagos', *Nigerian Journal of Economic and Social Studies*, vol. 20, November 1978.

FAO, 'Agricultural Credit in the Near East and the Mediterranean Basin', Report on the FAO Seminar on Agricultural Credit for Selected Countries, FAO, Rome, 1973.

FAO, 'Agricultural Credit in Africa', Report on the FAO/Finland Regional Seminar on Agricultural Credit in Africa, FAO, Rome, 1974.

FAO, 'Agricultural Credit in Asia', Report on the FAO Regional Seminar for Asia on Agricultural Credit for Small Farmers, FAO, Rome, 1975.

FAO, *Report on the World Conference on Credit for Farmers in Developing Countries*, Rome, 1975.

FAO, 'SACRED and Rural Development', Report of the FAO, Seminar on Harnessing the Financial System in Support of Rural Development, 22 July–12 Aug. 1981, Pune, India.

FAO, *Report of the AFRACA/EACACT Seminar on Resource Mobilisation for Rural Development*, 30 Jan.–10 Feb. 1984, Rome.

FAO, *Report of the Third Consultation on the Scheme for Agricultural Credit Development*, Rome, 1985.

FAO, 'Crop Insurance – Its Place in Development', Report of Expert Consultation, Rome 16–18 Sept. 1986.

FAO/APRACA, *Mobilisation of Rural Savings in Selected Countries in Asia and Pacific*, Bangkok, 1985.

FAO/APRACA, *Regional Seminar on Monitoring and Evaluation of Performance of Agricultural Credit Institutions in Asia and the Pacific*, Pattaya, Thailand, 9–13 December 1985.

Friedman, Milton, 'Controls of Interest Rates Paid by Banks', *Journal of Money, Credit and Banking*, 2, (1 February) 1970.

Fry, Maxwell J., 'National Saving, Financial Saving and Interest-Rate Policy in 14 Asian Developing Economies', paper prepared for the International Symposium on the Mobilization of Personal Savings in Developing Countries, Yaounde, Cameroun, 10–15 December, 1984.

Galbraith, John Kenneth, 'The Role of Agricultural Credit in Agricultural Development', *Proceedings of the International Conference on Agricultural and Co-operative Credit*, vol. 1, University of California, Berkeley, 1952.

Ghatak, Subrata, *Rural Money Markets in India*, Macmillan, New Delhi, 1976.

Giovannini, Alberto, 'The Interest Elasticity of Savings in Developing Countries: The Existing Evidence', *World Development*, 11, 7, July 1983.

Giovannini, Alberto, 'Saving and the Real Interest Rate in LDCs', *Journal of Development Economics*, August 1985.

Gonzalez-Vega, Claudio, 'Interest Rate Policies, Agricultural Credit and Income Distribution in Latin America', Second International Conference on the Financial Development of Latin America and the Caribbean. Caraballeda, Venezuela, April 1981.

Gonzalez-Vega, Claudio, *Strengthening Agricultural Banking and Credit Systems in Latin America and the Caribbean*, FAO, Rome, May 1986.

Grewal, H. S., 'An Evaluation of Research on Rural Financial Markets in India', PhD Dissertation, Department of Agricultural Economics and Rural Sociology, Ohio State University, Columbus, Ohio, 1982.

129

Grima, Begashaw, 'The Economic Role of Traditional Savings and Credit Institutions in Ethiopia', *Economics and Sociology Occasional Paper No. 456*, Ohio State University, Feb. 1978.

Gupta, Anil K., 'Banking in Backward Regions: Banks – NGO – Poor Interface: Alternatives for Action', Indian Institute of Management, Ahmedabad, India, *Working Paper, No. 675*, May 1987.

Holst, Jurgen U., 'The Role of Moneylenders, Traditional Savings and Credit Associations and Indigenous Bankers in the Mobilisation of Savings', Third United Nations International Symposium on the Mobilization of Personal Savings in Developing Countries, Paris, 1984.

Homer, Sidney, *History of Interest Rates*, 2nd edn, Rutgers University Press, New Brunswick, NJ, 1977.

Howell, John, (ed.), *Borrowers and Lenders: Rural Financial Markets and Institutions in Developing Countries*, Overseas Development Institute, London, 1980.

International Fund for Agricultural Development, *The Role of Rural Credit Projects in Reaching the Poor, IFAD's Experience*, IFAD Special Studies Series, vol. 1, Tycooly Publishing, Oxford, 1985.

International Fund for Agricultural Development, Monitoring and Evaluation. Guiding Principles, Rome, 1984.

International Labour Office, *Group-based Savings and Credit for the Rural Poor*, papers and proceedings of a workshop Bogra (Bangladesh), 6–10 Nov. 1983, ILO 1984.

Iqbal, Farrukh, 'The demand and supply of funds among agricultural households in India', in Inderjit Singh (ed.), *Agricultural Household Models*, Johns Hopkins University Press, 1986.

Kim, Sung-Hoon, *Rural Savings Mobilization: the Asian Experience*, paper presented at the Third United Nations International Symposium on the Mobilization of Personal Savings in Developing Countries, Yaounde, 10–15 Dec. 1984.

Kwadwo, Boakye-Dankwa, 'A Review of the Farm Loan Repayment Problem in Low Income Countries', *Economics and Sociology Occasional Paper No. 582*, Ohio State University, Feb. 1979.

Lanyi, Anthony, and Rusdu Saracoglu, 'Interest rate policies in developing countries', *Occasional Paper No. 22*, International Monetary Fund, Washington DC, 1983.

Lavington, *The English Capital Market*, Methuen & Co., London, 1934.

Lele, U. J., *The Design of Rural Development: Lessons from Africa*, Johns Hopkins University Press, Baltimore, 1975.

Levitsky, Jacob, and Rang N. Prasad, 'Credit guarantee schemes for small and medium enterprises', *World Bank Technical Paper No. 58*, Industry and Finance Series, Feb. 1987.

Lipton, M., 'Agricultural Finance and Rural Credit in Poor Countries', *World Development*, 4, 7, 1976, pp. 543–53.

Lipton, M., *Why Poor People Stay Poor*, Harvard University Press, Cambridge, Massachusetts, 1977.

Lipton, M., 'Agricultural Risk, Rural Credit and Inefficiency of Inequality', in Roumasset, J. A., J. Boussard and I. Singh (eds.), *Risk, Uncertainty and Agricultural Development*, SEARCA, Agricultural Development Council, New York, 1979.

Long, M. G., 'Why peasant farmers borrow', *American Journal of Agricultural Economics*, 50, 4, 1968, pp. 991–1008.

Mckinnon, Ronald I., *Money and Capital in Economic Development*, The Brookings Institution, Washington, 1973.

McNamara, Robert S., *Address to the Board of Governors of the World Bank Group*, IBRD, Washington DC, September 1973.

Mampally, P., 'Innovations in Banking: The Indian Experience', *Domestic Finance Studies no.66*, Public and Private Finance Division, World Bank, Dec. 1980.

Mauri, Arnaldo, 'The potential for savings and financial innovation in Africa', *Savings and Development*, 7, 4, 1983, pp. 310–37.

Mauri, Arnaldo, and Clara Caselli, *Financial Evolution and the Role of Central Banks in Africa*, paper presented at symposium on National Financial Policies and Capital Formation in Africa, African Centre for Monetary Studies, Cairo, July 1984.

Meyer, Richard L., 'Current issues in agricultural finance: interest rates and savings mobilization', in *Proceedings of Workshop on Small Farmer Development and Credit Policy, Kathmandu, Nepal, June 1981*, pp. 209–14.

Meyer, Richard L., *Rural Deposit Mobilization: An Alternative Approach for Developing Rural Financial Markets*, paper presented at the ID/IFAD Experts Meeting on Small Farmer Credit, Rome. Department of Agricultural Economics and Rural Sociology, Ohio State University, June 1985.

Meyer, Richard L., *Deposit Mobilization for Rural Lending*, paper at the Third Technical Consultation on the Scheme for Agricultural Credit Development (SACRED), FAO, Rome, 17–20 Sept. 1985.

Meyer, Richard L., and Emmanuel F. Esguerra, *Rural Deposit Mobilization in Asia*, paper presented at the XIX International Conference of Agricultural Economists, Malaga, Spain. Department of Agricultural Economics and Rural Sociology, Ohio State University, 1985.

Meyer, Richard L., and C. G. Vega, *Rural Deposit Mobilization in Developing Nations*, Development and Rural Areas, Göttingen University, Germany, Jan. 1986, pp. 9–11.

Mikesell, Raymond J., & James E. Zinser, 'The nature of the savings function in developing countries: A survey of the theoretical and empirical literature', *Journal of Economic Literature*, 11, 1, 1973, pp. 1–26.

Millard, Long, 'Interest rates and the structure of agricultural credit markets', *Oxford Economic Papers*, July 1968.

131

Miller, Leonard F., *Agricultural Credit and Finance in Africa*, The Rockefeller Foundation, New York, 1975.

Mittendorf, H. J., 'Mobilization of personal savings for agricultural and rural development in Africa', *Mondes en Developpement*, Tome 13, no. 50/51, 1985, pp. 275–91.

Mittendorf, H. J., *Promotion of Viable Rural Financial Systems for Agricultural Development*, FAO, Rome, 1986.

Mollett, J. A., *Planning for Agricultural Development*, Croom Helm, London, 1984.

Nicholas, M. S. O., *Strengthening Agricultural Credit Systems in African Countries*, Eighth Regular Meeting of the Association of African Central Banks, Arusha, Tanzania, 8–12 Aug. 1983.

Nisbet, Charles T., 'Interest rates and imperfect competition in the informal credit market of rural Chile', *Economic Development and Cultural Change*, Oct. 1967.

Ong, Marcia L., Dale W. Adams, and I. J. Singh, 'Voluntary Rural Savings Capacities in Taiwan, 1960–70', *American Journal of Agricultural Economics*, 58, 3, 1976.

Oxby, Clare, 'Farmer Groups in Cameroon: Some Experiments in Credit Delivery', ODI, London, Agricultural Administration Unit, *Discussion Paper No. 7*, Nov. 81.

OXFAM, *A Manual of Credit and Savings for the Poor of Developing Countries*, Oxford, 1987.

Padmanabhan, K. P., *Rural Financial Intermediation: Changing Perceptions*, Shubhada-Saraswat, Pune, India, 1986.

Padmanabhan, K. P., 'Why farmers default on loans', *CERES*, FAO Review, No. 109 (19, 1), Jan.–Feb. 1986.

Padmanabhan, K. P., 'Giving credit where due', *Ceres*, No. 115 (20, 1), Jan.–Feb. 1987.

Pani, P. K., 'Cultivators' demand for credit: a cross-section analysis', *International Economic Review*, 7, 2, 1966, pp. 176–203.

Patrick, Hugh T., 'Financial development and economic growth in developing countries', *Economic Development and Cultural Change*, 14, 2, Jan. 1966.

Penny, D. H., 'Farm credit policy in the early stages of agricultural development', *Australian Journal of Agricultural Economics*, 12, 1, 1968, pp. 32–45.

Quinones, B. R., *An Overview of Agricultural Credit Systems in Selected Asian Countries*, APRACA, Bangkok, 1985.

Rahman, Farhana Haque, 'The potential for domestic savings', *CERES*, FAO Review, 19, 1, Jan.–Feb. 1986.

Rangarajan, C., 'Innovations in banking: the Indian experience. Impact on deposits and credit', *Domestic Finance Studies 63*, Public and Private Finance Division, World Bank, 1980.

Reserve Bank of India, 'All India rural credit survey', vol.II, *The General Report*, Bombay, 1954.

Reserve Bank of India, *Report of the All-India Rural Credit Review Committee*, Bombay, 1969.

Reserve Bank of India, *Report of the Expert Group on State Enactments Having a Bearing on Commercial Banks Lending to Agriculture*, Bombay, 1971.

Reserve Bank of India, *Report of the Study Team on Overdues of Co-operative Credit Institutions*, Bombay, July 1974.

Reserve Bank of India, *Report of the Committee to Review Arrangements for Institutional Credit for Agriculture and Rural Development*, Bombay, 1981

Reserve Bank of India, *Reserve Bank of India and Rural Credit*, Rural Planning and Credit Department, Bombay 1985.

Robert, Bruce L. Jr. 'Agricultural Credit Co-operatives, Rural Development and Agrarian Politics in Madras, 1893–1937', *Indian Economics and Social History Review*, 16, 2, 1979.

Roberts, R. A. J., 'Personnel deficiencies in agricultural banking systems in developing countries', *Savings and Development*, 2, 1, 1978, pp. 20–42.

Roe, Alan R., 'Some theory concerning the role and failings of financial intermediation in less developed countries', *World Bank Staff Working Paper No. 338*, 1979.

Sacay, Orlando J., Meliza H. Agabin, and Chita Irene E. Tonchoco, *Small Farmer Credit Dilemma*, Central Bank of the Philippines, Manila, 1985.

Samaranayake, Tilak, 'Interest rate policies and economic development: the Sri Lankan experience since 1977', *Economic Review*, October 1986.

Sanderatne, Nimal, 'An analytical approach to loan defaults by small farmers', *Savings and Development*, 2, 4, 1978.

Schaefer-Kehnert, W., and J. D. von Pischke, 'Agricultural credit policy in developing countries', *Savings and Development*, 1, 1986, pp. 5–30.

Schultz, Theodore W., *Transforming Traditional Agriculture*, Yale University Press, New Haven, 1964.

Seibel, H. D., 'Savings for development – a linkage model for informal and formal financial markets', *Quarterly Journal of International Agriculture*, 24, 4, Oct.–Dec. 1985, pp 390–8.

Shaw, E. S., *Financial Deepening in Economic Development*, Oxford University Press, New York, 1973.

Sturm, Peter H., 'Determinants of savings: theory and evidence'. *OECD Economic Studies*, (Autumn) 1983.

Thingalaya, N. K., 'Innovations in banking: the syndicates experience',

Domestic Finance Studies No. 46, Department of Development Economics, World Bank, Jan. 1978.

Tun Wai, U., 'Role of financial markets in development', *Finafrica Bulletin*, 3, 3, 1976, pp. 91–105.

Tun Wai, U., 'Strategies and policies to stimulate and develop capital markets', *Savings and Development*, 1, 2, 1977, pp. 57–78.

Tun Wai, U., 'Interest rates outside the organized money markets of under-developed countries', *IMF Staff Papers*, vol. 6, Nov. 1957.

United Nations, *Savings for Development*, report of the Third International Symposium on the Mobilization of Personal Savings in Developing Countries, Yaounde, Cameroun, 10–14 Dec. 1984, New York, 1985.

US Agency for International Development, *Spring Review of Small Farmer Credit*, vols. 1–20, Washington, 1973.

US Agency for International Development, 'A synthesis of AID experience: small-farmer credit, 1973–1985', *AID Evaluation Special Study No. 41*, October 1985.

Vasthoff, J., *Small Farm Credit and Development: Some Experiences in East Africa with Special Reference to Kenya*, Weltforum, Munich, 1968.

Virmani, Arvind, 'The nature of credit markets in developing countries – a framework for policy analysis', *World Bank Staff Working Paper No. 524*, World Bank, 1982.

Vogel, Robert C., 'Rural financial market performance: implications of low delinquency rates', *American Journal of Agricultural Economics*, 63, 1, 1981, pp. 58–65.

Vogel, Robert C., and Paul Burkett, 'Mobilizing small-scale savings: approaches, costs and benefits', *Industry and Finance Series Volume 15*, The World Bank, 1986.

Von Pischke, John D., 'The pitfalls of specialized farm credit insitutions in low income countries', *Development Digest*, 18, 3, July 1980.'

Von Pischke, John D., Dale W. Adams, and Gordon Donald (eds.), *Rural Financial Markets in Developing Countries – Their Use and Abuse*, Johns Hopkins University Press, Baltimore, 1983.

Von Pischke, John D., and John Rouse, 'Selected Successful Experiences in Agricultural Credit and Rural Finance in Africa', *Savings and Development*, 7, 1, 1983.

Walinsky, J. Louis, *The Planning and Execution of Economic Development*, McGraw Hill, New York, 1963.

Wells, R. J. G., *The Informal Rural Credit Market in Peninsular Malaysia*, Fakult: Ekonomi and Pentadbiran, University of Malaysia, 1980.

World Bank, *Agricultural Credit-Sector Policy Paper*, World Bank, Washington DC, 1975.

Wortman, Sterling, 'Food and Agriculture', *Scientific American*, September 1976.

Zambia, Republic of, *Zambia Agricultural Finance Markets: Appraisal of Recent Performance and Prospects*, June 1983.

Index

Robert, Bruce L. 34
Rockefeller Foundation 12
Role of credit 6ff
Rotating Savings and Credit
  Associations 45, 88
Rural credit policies 10ff
Rural Credit Programme, Jamaica
  72
Rural Credit Programme, Sri Lanka
  75
Rural financial markets 25ff
Rural financial institutions 96ff
Rural savings 38, 39

Sanderatne, Nimal 67
Savings (general) 27, 38, 39, 40, 41,
  42, 44
Savings Movement, Zimbabwe 42
Schools' Savings Scheme, Mauritius
  41
Schultz, T.W. 6, 18
Self-employed Womens' Co-
  operative, India 41
Self-supporting Farmers'
  Development Programme, Jamaica
  72
Shakespeare 6, 109, 120
Shingkan Buddhist Sutra 31
Sierra Leone 86
Small farmers 19, 29, 34, 51
Smith, Adam 37
Spring Review 12, 13, 19, 66, 89, 90
Sri Lanka 30, 42, 45, 66, 67, 71, 75
Structure of financial institutions 31ff
Studies, Innovation, Development
  and Experimentations Unit,
  Bangladesh 79
Subsidies 83
Sudan 13
Sung-Hoon, Kim 38
Symposium of Rural Credit 89
Syndicate Agriculture Foundation,
  India 55

Syndicate Bank, India 41, 55

Taiwan 10, 11, 17, 35, 40, 42, 43
Tanzania 33
Technical Board for Agricultural
  Credit, Philippines 83, 114
Technology 78, 79, 111
Thailand 25, 71
Timberlake, Lloyd x
Togo 92
Transaction costs, administrative costs
  41, 45, 53, 56
Tringo Maria, Peru 46
Tunisia 57
Turkey 32, 50

Uganda 13, 42
UN Symposium on Mobilisation of
  Personal Savings 38, 92
USAID 11, 12, 66, 73, 78, 89, 118, 119

Vietnam 13
Village Banks, Egypt 83
Village seed bank scheme, India 51
Vogel, Robert C. 42, 76
Volunteer Vikas Vahini, India 56
Von Pischke, J.D. 33

Walinsky, L.J. 10
Weaver, Warren 96
Wolamo Agricultural Development
  Unit, Ethiopia 48
World Bank 12, 15, 67, 72, 111,
  118
Wortman, S. 17
Women's Savings Club, Zimbabwe 41

Yaoundé 92
Yunus, Prof 60

Zambia 33, 80, 106
Zimbabwe 33, 41, 42, 81
Zimbabwe Grain Marketing Board 81

138